PRAISE FOR

The Robe and the Sword

"Sonia Faleiro is a master of narrative reportage, illuminating every topic she touches. This book that connects colonial fault lines, broken economies, the scourge of Islamophobia, and extremism is one that only Faleiro can write. Pay heed: It is the story of our broken world."

—FATIMA BHUTTO,
author of *The Hour of the Wolf* and co-editor of *Gaza: The Story of a Genocide*

"With sharp insight and deep humanity, Sonia Faleiro's *The Robe and the Sword* traces the long and uneasy bond between Buddhism and political power, offering a vital portrait of how faith, identity, and resistance are being redefined across the region."

—THANT MYINT-U,
author of *Peacemaker: U Thant and the Forgotten Quest for a Just World* and *The Hidden History of Burma: Race, Capitalism, and the Crisis of Democracy in the 21st Century*

"With intellectual resourcefulness and rigor, Sonia Faleiro describes one of nationalism's most insidious and least-noticed mutations. Briskly and accessibly, *The Robe and the Sword* charts the complex social-economic shifts that make even an ancient spiritual tradition devoted to renunciation hospitable to modern fanaticism."

—PANKAJ MISHRA,
author of *The World After Gaza*

"Sonia Faleiro's *The Robe and the Sword* is a must-read piece of the puzzle of rising religious and ethnonationalism worldwide. This meticulous reporting and analysis offers a sorely needed broad take on Buddhist extremism's impact on some of the world's most vulnerable people. Faleiro is one of our best journalists and thinkers. Unflinching in pursuing narratives that disrupt our established ways of seeing, she insists that we enlarge our field of vision to see the critical historical and contemporary connections beyond national borders."

—V.V. GANESHANANTHAN,
author of *Brotherless Night*

The Robe and the Sword

COLUMBIA GLOBAL REPORTS
NEW YORK

The Robe and the Sword

How Buddhist Extremism Is Shaping Modern Asia

Sonia Faleiro

Dharamshala
Delhi
India
Mumbai
Bengaluru
(Bangalore)
Tamil
Nadu
Jaffna
Sri Lanka
Digana
Colombo
Aluthgama

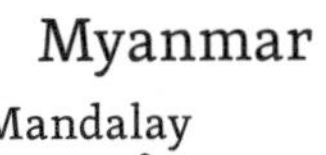
Myanmar
Mandalay
Kyaukse
Meiktila
Rakhine State
Myawaddy
Mae Sot
Thailand
Bangkok
Pattani

The Robe and the Sword
How Buddhist Extremism Is Shaping Modern Asia

Published by Columbia Global Reports
91 Claremont Avenue, Suite 515
New York, NY 10027
globalreports.columbia.edu

Library of Congress Cataloging-in-Publication Data
Names: Faleiro, Sonia, author.
Title: The robe and the sword : how Buddhist extremism is shaping modern Asia / by Sonia Faleiro.
Description: New York : Columbia Global Reports, [2025] | Includes bibliographical references.
Identifiers: LCCN 2025012996 (print) | LCCN 2025012997 (ebook) | ISBN 9781967190003 (paperback) | ISBN 9781967190010 (ebook)
Subjects: LCSH: Buddhism and politics—Southeast Asia. | Radicalism—Religious aspects—Buddhism. | Buddhism—Relations—Islam. | Nationalism—Sri Lanka—Religious aspects—Buddhism. | Nationalism—Burma—Religious aspects—Buddhism. | Nationalism—Thailand—Religious aspects—Buddhism.
Classification: LCC BQ4570.S7 F35 2025 (print) | LCC BQ4570.S7 (ebook) | DDC 294.3/372—dc23/eng/20250613
LC record available at https://lccn.loc.gov/2025012996
LC ebook record available at https://lccn.loc.gov/2025012997

Book design by Kelly Winton
Map design by Jeffrey L. Ward
Author photograph by Robin Christian

Printed in the United States of America

For Indira,
May we always travel together

CONTENTS

India

- **Narendra Modi:** Prime minister of India, a lifelong member of the Hindu nationalist Rashtriya Swayamsevak Sangh (RSS), and leader of the Bharatiya Janata Party (BJP), known for his anti-Muslim policies.
- **Rashtriya Swayamsevak Sangh (RSS):** A Hindu nationalist organization founded in 1925 that inspires the ideology of the BJP, with a history of anti-Muslim rhetoric and deep influence on Indian politics.
- **Arya Samaj:** A Hindu reformist movement advocating a return to Vedic principles, often seen as a precursor to modern Hindu nationalist ideologies.
- **Khilafat Movement:** An early-twentieth-century Muslim-led campaign in India against British colonial rule, merging religious and political resistance.

Sri Lanka

- **Galagoda Aththe Gnanasara:** Ultra-nationalist monk and leader of the Bodu Bala Sena.
- **Bodu Bala Sena (BBS):** An ultra-nationalist organization led by Galagoda Aththe Gnanasara and militant Buddhist monks in Sri Lanka, known for its anti-Muslim campaigns and nationalist rhetoric.
- **Rauff Hakeem:** Leader of Sri Lanka's largest Muslim political party and a vocal critic of the Bodu Bala Sena.

- **Rajapaksa Brothers:** A powerful political dynasty accused of authoritarianism and fostering nationalist policies, often linked to ethno-nationalist mobilization during and after the civil war.
- **Anagarika Dharmapala:** A Sri Lankan Buddhist revivalist who framed Buddhism as central to Sinhalese identity.

Myanmar

- **Than Shwe:** Former head of Myanmar's military junta, responsible for widespread persecution of ethnic and religious minorities, including the Rohingya.
- **Min Aung Hlaing:** Senior general and leader of Myanmar's junta during the Rohingya genocide.
- **Aung San Suu Kyi:** Former leader of the opposition who played a crucial role in the country's transition from military junta to partial democracy; state counselor of Myanmar.
- **Ashin Wirathu:** Leader of the 969 movement and Ma Ba Tha, infamous for inciting hatred against Myanmar's Rohingya population.
- **Abbot Zero:** Dissident monk opposing Buddhist extremism in Myanmar, once a follower of Ashin Wirathu but now critical of his violent ideology.
- **969 movement:** A nationalist Buddhist movement in Myanmar opposing Muslim populations, led by Wirathu.
- **Ma Ba Tha:** Organization for the Protection of Race and Religion, a more formal and politically influential successor to 969.

Thailand

- **Saharat Sukhamla:** A Thai activist and former monk who advocates for the monarchy to avoid interfering in religious practice.
- **Sulak Sivaraksa:** Thai social critic and engaged Buddhist, often critical of nationalism and monarchy.
- **Maha Vajiralongkorn:** Thailand's current king, whose reign began in 2016 and reflects the complexities of balancing modernity and tradition within Thai society.
- **Thai Military Junta:** A powerful entity in Thai politics, influencing governance and suppressing dissent, often with the tacit support of Buddhist clergy.
- **Wat Phra Dhammakaya:** A controversial Thai Buddhist movement often described as reformist, but criticized for commercializing Buddhism and promoting a cult of personality around its leaders.
- **Phra Dhammachayo:** Controversial abbot of Wat Phra Dhammakaya, accused of promoting a wealth-focused interpretation of Buddhism.
- **Santi Asoke:** An alternative Buddhist sect rejecting consumerism and embracing sustainability.
- **Dhammananda Bhikkhuni:** The first Thai woman in centuries to be ordained as a Buddhist monk, she is the abbot of the Songdhammakalyani Monastery, the first all-female temple in Thailand, located in Nakhon Pathom near Bangkok.

Tibet

- **His Holiness the Fourteenth Dalai Lama:** Spiritual leader of Tibetan Buddhism and former political head of Tibet. Following the 1959 Tibetan uprising, he fled to India, where he established a government in exile in Dharamshala.
- **Lhakpa Tsering:** A Tibetan activist who attempted self-immolation in 2007 against China's occupation of his homeland.
- **Tibetan self-immolations:** A movement involving over 150 individuals since 2009.

Introduction
India

In the summer of 2023, I arrived in Dharamshala, a town cradled in the shadow of the Dhauladhar mountains and celebrated as the home of the Dalai Lama, the Tibetan spiritual leader. The place hadn't changed much since my last visit almost two decades earlier. The roads were still a patchwork of uneven asphalt and dirt, and the monkeys, sharp-eyed and curious, perched on rooftops and shop awnings as they always had. Tibetan monks in maroon robes filled the streets. Despite the relentless hum of traffic, Dharamshala had a rare stillness. The hills seemed to absorb the noise. Prayer flags flickered in the breeze, each rustle a reminder of something enduring.

But beneath the surface, the Buddhism practiced across Asia has shifted. While still widely seen as a peaceful, nonviolent philosophy, it has been weaponized, in some quarters, in the service of nationalism, and in support of governments embracing a global trend toward majoritarianism and autocracy.

In countries like Sri Lanka and Myanmar, where the conservative Theravada strain predominates, monks have emerged as central figures in movements that promote sectarian hatred, abandoning the teachings of the Buddha in favor of a more common and earthly goal: political power. My journey to Dharamshala and across other parts of the Buddhist world was driven by a need to understand how this transformation had occurred.

I had come to Dharamshala to meet Lhakpa Tsering, a Tibetan refugee who gained international attention in 2006 when he set himself on fire outside the Taj Mahal Hotel in Mumbai in a high-profile act of protest timed to coincide with a visit from Chinese Premier Hu Jintao. Photographs of Lhakpa, flames leaping from his jeans and combat boots, dominated India's front pages. Then twenty-three, Lhakpa was a master's student in Bangalore, newly involved in the Free Tibet movement. His decision to protest by harming himself while sparing others struck me at the time as a profoundly Buddhist act.

I was only a little older than Lhakpa when it happened, working as a magazine journalist in Mumbai. India was on the brink of something new. It had been more than a decade since the sweeping economic reforms of 1991 had loosened the grip of state control and opened the doors to a market-driven economy. By 2006, the changes were visible everywhere: The skyline was rising, the economy was humming, and a new middle class was finding its feet. For some of us, the future felt full of possibility.

Britain's two-century colonial occupation had devastated India not just economically but socially. It had deepened religious divides that, though they had always existed, had never before caused such bloodshed. The divisions reached their climax in 1947, when India was cleaved into Hindu-majority India and Muslim-majority Pakistan, and Pakistan itself was later divided between east and west, displacing millions who trekked across borders, clutching the few possessions they could carry.

In the aftermath, religious riots became a recurrent part of life in India. Muslims were often the targets, and later investigations revealed the instigating role of the Rashtriya Swayamsevak Sangh (RSS), a shadowy Hindu extremist group formed by upper-caste Hindus who drew inspiration from the European fascist movements of the 1930s. In 1948, a former member of the RSS assassinated Mahatma Gandhi accusing him of acting against Indian Hindu interests by negotiating with Indian Muslims, and the group was briefly banned.

Every day, paunchy, middle-aged men in khaki shorts lined up in the park near my home, gripping batons, their knees pumping out of time like a faltering chorus line. Yet beneath the almost comic surface was something formidable: a machine fueled by the conviction that India belonged to Hindus alone. By 2023, the RSS claimed four million members, and wielded near-absolute power through its political wing, the Bharatiya Janata Party, led by the country's Prime Minister Narendra Modi, a lifelong adherent.

Even as Hindu nationalism surged, I kept returning to a different strand of India's heritage, one rooted in the stories of my childhood. The first graphic novels I ever read were the Jataka tales, which tell the stories of the Buddha's past lives. They are filled with clever animals—elusive antelopes, trickster crocodiles, and wise monkeys. In school, my class took field trips to Bodh Gaya, the place where Siddhartha Gautama attained enlightenment under the Bodhi tree, becoming the Buddha. Symbols of the Buddha were everywhere, even on the Indian flag, where the wheel of the Dharma—set in motion with the Buddha's first sermon—holds pride of place.

 The idea of a young Siddhartha Gautama giving up luxury and comfort to search for the meaning of life resonated with newly independent India, many of whose families had resisted or actively fought British rule. Their political consciousness was further shaped by the decision of Jawaharlal Nehru, India's first prime minister, to embrace a policy of nonalignment during the Cold War. Like Siddhartha, a newly reborn India chose neither one established path nor the other, but instead decided to make its own way in the world.

Siddhartha was born in the village of Lumbini, on the borderlands of India and Nepal, likely in the fifth century BCE. According to some accounts, his mother, Maya, was traveling from Kapilavatsu, where the family lived, to her parental home, when she went into labor and gave birth in a garden. His father, Suddhodana, belonged to the Kshatriya, or warrior, caste and was a chieftain with king-like status. He was an indulgent parent to his only son, whom he raised in palatial homes filled with servants tasked with doing the boy's bidding.

It was a golden age of ideas. In Greece, Plato argued that rational inquiry was essential to grasping truth and achieving justice. In Persia, the sage Zoroaster introduced a radical vision centered on the cosmic struggle between truth and falsehood. And in India, the Vedic traditions that had established the iron grip of the caste system and the supremacy of upper caste Brahmins were being challenged by new systems of heterodox thought—among them Jainism and Buddhism. The revolutionary minds behind these extraordinary new ideas "sought change in the deepest reaches of their beings," observed the religious scholar Karen Armstrong. "[They] looked for greater inwardness in their spiritual lives, and tried to become one with a reality that transcended normal mundane conditions and categories. After this pivotal era, it was felt that only by reaching beyond their limits could human beings become most fully themselves."

Siddhartha's father considered these changes far too radical for his only son, and did everything he could to protect the boy from the reality of the world. According to Buddhist mythology, Siddhartha had reached the age of twenty-nine before he even laid eyes on an elderly person. Turning to his charioteer, Siddhartha wondered: "What kind of man is this, whose very hair is not as that of other men?" When he heard his servant's answer, Siddhartha replied, "Shame then be to life! Since the decay of every living being is notorious!"

Not long after, Siddhartha quietly slipped from his father's palace, saddled his beloved horse Kanthaka, and raced out of the city. Severing all contact with his family—including his wife and newborn child—he sought only the company of yogis and monks. He pursued meditation and asceticism and practiced extreme fasting, pushing his body to its limits. He was on a relentless quest to find the answer to human suffering and was willing to sacrifice everything to discover it. "Because of eating so little my limbs became like the jointed segments of vine stems or bamboo stems," he said, according to one early account of his life. "Because of eating so little my backside became like a camel's hoof. Because of eating so little the projections on my spine stood forth like corded beads."

Six years passed before he gained enlightenment. It was around 528 BCE, and as he sat deep in meditation under a Bodhi tree in the village of Bodh Gaya, he realized that neither the luxury he had rejected nor the deprivation he had embraced held the key to transcending humanity's trials. Instead, the path to enlightenment lay between extremes: the Middle Way. That was what he told his followers in his first-ever sermon as the Buddha.

The Buddha explained the insights he had gained as a result of becoming enlightened in the form of the Four Noble Truths. The first truth is that life is marked by dukkha, a term that can mean suffering, impermanence, and dissatisfaction. This suffering is caused by tanhā, the second truth, which refers to craving, thirst, or attachment. The third truth is that there is, in fact, an end to suffering, called nibbāna, and it marks the end of the cycle of rebirth. The fourth truth teaches the Noble Eightfold Path, a guide outlining the steps to end suffering and attain enlightenment, completing the cycle that begins with the recognition of suffering.

"The very format of the first sermon and its Four Noble Truths follows a medical model," noted the University of Oxford scholar Richard Gombrich. "Diagnosing the complaint, finding its cause, finding what would eliminate the cause, [and] prescribing the medicine to achieve that elimination."

Above all, one principle has come to define Buddhism in the eyes of the world: the foundational precept of ahimsa, or non-harming. The Sri Lankan monk Walpola Rahula, who taught at Northwestern University, defined the Buddha's ahimsa as an injunction not only to avoid harming another person but to *prevent* violence committed by others. "The Buddha not only taught non-violence and peace," Rahula wrote, "but he even went to the field of battle itself and intervened personally and prevented war."

Mahatma Gandhi famously embodied nonviolence in modern times. He responded to British colonial exploitation and violence with nonviolent noncooperation, known as satyagraha. Gandhi's methods included a 240-mile walk against unjust taxation and a 21-day fast. In the 1950s, Martin Luther King Jr. embraced Gandhi's philosophy of nonviolent resistance for the American Civil Rights Movement. "Christ showed us the way, and Gandhi in India showed us it could work," King declared during the Montgomery bus boycott in 1956.

Meanwhile, events in Asia were bringing Buddhism into sharper focus for the West. In 1959, as Chinese occupying forces tightened their grip on Tibet, the Fourteenth Dalai Lama made a dramatic escape on horseback across the Himalayas into India, capturing the world's attention and highlighting Tibet's struggle.

By the 1960s, Buddhist monks were showing Americans how to sit still. Meditation and chanting, once esoteric practices, became stand-ins for Buddhism itself in the Western imagination. The Dalai Lama's peaceful response to China's aggression, boosted by high-profile advocates like actor Richard Gere, cemented Buddhism's reputation as a philosophy of nonviolence and inner peace. For many disillusioned by materialism and in search of a more meaningful existence, it was exactly what they were looking for. But as the feminist writer and Buddhist bell hooks would later note, Buddhism's American makeover wasn't entirely innocent. "Many people see the contemplative traditions—specifically those from Asia—as being for privileged white people," she wrote, observing that the Western embrace of Buddhism often centered on the comforts of the materially secure.

Soon, Buddha statues were being sold next to crystals, incense, scented oils, and mindfulness apps. Buddhism had found its place in the wellness aisle. But something got lost in the translation. What had once been a radical philosophy of renunciation and interdependence began to resemble the very consumerism it was supposed to critique. Few of its new followers knew that a previous Dalai Lama, Thubten Gyatso, had founded a Tibetan army in 1913, or that rivalries between monasteries in Tibet occasionally led to monks taking up arms. Even the distinct traditions within Buddhism—Mahayana, Theravada, and Tantric—were smoothed into a single, marketable idea: Buddhism as balm.

Yet, for all its oversimplifications, the Western interpretation of Buddhism offered a compelling alternative to the stresses of modern life, promising something even more elusive now than it was several decades ago—serene acceptance in a world spinning wildly out of control.

By the 2000s, Buddhist outrage had taken more familiar forms. In Buddhist-majority nations like Sri Lanka and Myanmar—countries that, like India, share a history of colonial rule—nationalist groups were adopting strikingly similar tactics: fearmongering, militant organizing, and inciting violence. A strategy of communal division, rooted in colonial-era policies, was adapted to contemporary anxieties and used to terrorize fellow citizens.

In Sri Lanka, the saffron robes of Buddhist monks have become a fearsome symbol for the country's Muslim minority, as groups like the Bodu Bala Sena rally followers under the banner of "protecting" Buddhism. In Myanmar, similar robes adorn figures like Ashin Wirathu, who incited genocide against the Rohingya.

The monks leading these violent movements were driven not by a pursuit of nirvana in the next life, but by a quest for dominance in this one. Their actions, I came to understand, were shaped in part by historical forces such as colonialism, which introduced racial hierarchies and privileged certain religions over others. Economic inequality compounded these tensions, compelling the public to seek solace in religion and, in turn, granting monks disproportionate social and political influence. What emerged was a pattern that mirrors other parts of the world: violent nationalist movements gaining momentum at the expense of minorities, with those in power weaponizing a sense of victimhood to consolidate control.

Yet, these monks also illuminate a lesser-known dimension of Buddhism: its patriarchal structure. Across South and Southeast Asia—particularly within the Theravada tradition—male monks enjoy privileges systematically denied to women. In Sri Lanka, for instance, female monks are prohibited from receiving government-issued identity cards under pressure from the male clergy, barring them from voting, obtaining passports, or accessing public healthcare. In Tibet, nuns rarely gain access to secular education. And in Thailand, women can't be ordained as monks at all. They may take vows as nuns, but are often relegated to domestic labor within temple grounds. Figures like Wirathu—lionized by their followers, legitimized by their robes—make visible the hierarchies of voice and power: who is elevated, who is heard, and who is silenced. Their rise shows how nationalism entwines with masculine ideologies to reinforce male dominance—within the Sangha, and far beyond it.

Alongside this deeply gendered imbalance, acts of radical defiance continue to flourish. Buddhist nuns have emerged as some of the most courageous challengers of both political repression and religious patriarchy. In Tibet, many have protested Chinese rule at great personal risk—some have been imprisoned; others have disappeared. A few have self-immolated, drinking kerosene and setting themselves alight, their bodies wrapped in barbed wire to prevent rescue.

Elsewhere, resistance takes a different form. At the Druk Amitabha Mountain Nunnery overlooking Kathmandu, Nepal, the so-called "Kung Fu Nuns" begin each day by swapping their robes for martial arts uniforms. "Kung Fu helps us to break gender barriers and develop inner confidence," Jigme Rabsal Lhamo told *The New York Times*. "It also helps to take care of others during crises." In Dharamshala, activism spills beyond the monastery walls. Nuns work in schools and hospitals, lead litter-picking drives, and educate laypeople about climate change. It was here that I met Tenzin Kunsel, who teaches Buddhist philosophy at the Dolma Ling Nunnery and Institute of Buddhist Dialectics. The first Buddhist nun in India to earn the *geshema* degree—the equivalent of a PhD in Tibetan Buddhism—Kunsel achieved a milestone that was only formally made available to women in 2012. She told me one reason she left Tibet was that nuns in Lhasa are not given an education. Her sister is also a nun, she said, and has only ever been taught prayers. For Kunsel, education is progress—and defiance.

At the Library of Tibetan Works and Archives, the scholar Geshe Lhakdor offered a stark assessment of the moral crisis confronting the Buddhist clergy. Paraphrasing Martin Luther King Jr., he said, "I don't feel sad when bad people do bad things. I feel sad when good people don't do anything." The real danger, he explained, wasn't just the extremists—but the deafening silence of the majority. When I asked why violent monks continued to be recognized within the religious fold, Lhakdor was unsparing: "You become a monk or a nun because you choose to. And if you break the rules, there's nothing anyone can do." His voice carried a note of weary resignation. "It's very, very complicated," he sighed.

My encounters in Dharamshala pointed to a growing realization within Buddhist communities: that in our interconnected and fragile world, merely refraining from harm is no longer enough. The crises we face demand a more engaged Buddhism—one that responds to violence not only with contemplation, but with action.

Lhakpa, the young Tibetan refugee, had once captured global attention with his act of self-immolation. Now in his forties, he was married, a father, and running a small café high in the hills of Dharamshala. His resistance had taken on a different shape: he wrote and directed plays about Tibetan refugee life. The fire hadn't visibly disfigured Lhakpa, but he told me he sometimes still felt a twinge of pain where his skin had burned. As we sat in his café eating dumplings, he asked if I knew the story of the Buddha and the starving tigress.

In the story, the Buddha, as a prince, encounters a starving tigress and her cubs. "Her sunken eyes and her emaciated belly betokened her hunger, and she was regarding her own offspring as food." Seeing that the tigress is too weak to hunt, the prince leaps from a cliff, offering his body as a sacrifice. "I will kill my miserable body by casting it down into the precipice, and with my corpse I shall preserve the tigress from killing her young ones and the young ones from dying by the teeth of their mother."

The moral of the tale is clear: Though the Buddha abhorred even self-inflicted violence, such sacrifice can be justified if it serves the greater good. "To sacrifice your body for the well-being of another," Lhakpa told me, "is the highest form of nonviolent action."

At that moment, I understood: For Lhakpa, self-immolation wasn't merely an act of protest; it was the living continuation of an ancient Buddhist tradition of profound sacrifice. His willingness to surrender his body echoed the transcendent generosity the Buddha showed the starving tigress. Yet, stories like this had also become ammunition for violent Buddhists who justified aggression by claiming their actions were similarly motivated by the greater good—to protect Buddhists, and Buddhism itself.

As I left, Lhakpa stacked our teacups and wiped down the table. The prayer flags kept fluttering above the hills. In the town below, the monks walked as they always had. But something had shifted. The silence no longer sounded like peace.

Part One

Sri Lanka

Army of Buddhist Power

Later that summer, I drove south from the Sri Lankan capital, Colombo, to meet Fazeena Fihar, a Muslim tutor who had survived a harrowing ordeal. Her village, Adhikarigoda, was a breezy hamlet of whitewashed houses and fragrant trees, where the sky mirrored the brilliant blue of a Sri Lankan magpie. Fihar, a tall woman of forty-one, wore a hijab and had sharply defined cheekbones. As she ushered me into a living room where the sofa was still wrapped in plastic, I noticed that walls were conspicuously bare—no family photographs, no academic certificates, none of the proud displays so common in Sri Lankan homes. I didn't have to ask why.

In 2014, a mob had ransacked Fihar's house, tramping through the family's mango orchard, torching their tuk-tuk, and setting fire to their belongings. Beds, tables, crockery and curtains, photo albums and schoolbooks, even a doll's house—were reduced to ashes. Everything around me, from ceiling to floor, was new, rebuilt over many difficult years.

Fihar brought tea in a delicate white cup but refused to sit. She stood with her gaze fixed on the open window overlooking the empty road.

"Did you see the videos?" she asked. "It was purely against Muslims. 'Don't go to their shops. Don't eat their food.'"

Fihar was referring to a speech by Galagoda Aththe Gnanasara, a Buddhist monk with a spiteful tongue. By 2023, Sri Lanka had no shortage of controversial clergy, but Gnanasara stood apart. His exploits were legendary: arrests for drunk driving and hit-and-runs, an appetite for luxury cars and coteries of bodyguards.

Understanding Sri Lanka's complex religious landscape is critical to making sense of Gnanasara's rise. In this island nation of 22 million, Buddhism is not merely a faith but a cornerstone of national identity for the Sinhalese majority, who make up about 75 percent of the population. The constitution itself grants Buddhism "the foremost place," creating a delicate balance—or imbalance—between secular governance and religious preference, and often making the country's religious minorities, including Tamil Hindus (12.6 percent), Muslims (9.7 percent), and Christians (7.4 percent), feel like second-class citizens.

The reverence afforded to monks may help explain why figures like Gnanasara are allowed to remain in the clergy despite committing repeated transgressions that, according to the Vinaya—the monastic code of conduct established by the Buddha himself—should automatically result in disrobing. These include engaging in sexual intercourse, stealing something of value, intentionally killing a human being or encouraging another to do so, and falsely claiming to be enlightened. Yet, Gnanasara has managed to reinvent himself, over and over again. His origin story is the first clue as to how.

Gnanasara was born in 1975 in Galle, a city on the southwestern coast of Sri Lanka, to a family of very modest means. He has several siblings and a close relationship with his elderly mother. According to him, he began his monastic life as a forest monk. Forest monks live in cave-like dwellings in dry tropical forests and devote themselves to rigorous mental and moral discipline. Anyone familiar with Gnanasara's voracious appetite for material pleasures would find this version of events difficult to believe. According to him, within a few years he had exchanged the solitude of the forest for the bustle of Colombo, where he enrolled at a monastic university. Official records show that this was when his frequent run-ins with the law became public. His offenses ranged from drunk driving to threatening a woman, and cast doubt on how much studying he actually did. In Colombo, a different version of Gnanasara's past circulated—one in which, far from being called to religion, he was a small-time thug who embraced the robes to escape prison time.

In the mid-2000s, Gnanasara joined the Jathika Hela Urumaya (JHU), the world's first political party formed entirely of Buddhist monks. He stood for parliamentary elections, which he lost. Over time, he developed a close relationship with the Rajapaksas—Sri Lanka's most powerful and polarizing political dynasty—whom the Crisis Group once described as "aggressively Sinhala nationalist, family-centered, and authoritarian." The Rajapaksas were among the most prominent supporters of monks like Gnanasara, but they were not alone. "Regardless of who is in power," Ambika Satkunanathan, the former commissioner of the Human Rights Commission of Sri Lanka, told me, "all the Sinhalese parties are a little bit scared of the monks. Before announcing a new policy, they always go to the monks to explain it to them and get their support. Whatever power the monks have is what politicians have given them."

In 2012, Gnanasara cofounded the Bodu Bala Sena (BBS), or Army of Buddhist Power, which claimed it would protect the Buddhist majority from threats posed by minority religious groups. Among its key demands were preferential treatment for Buddhist students, and a ban on Muslim practices such as the slaughter of cattle for religious rituals and the certification of products as halal. Gnanasara and his BBS cohort hosted rallies that drew thousands and leveraged their social media following—which grew to over 100,000 on Facebook alone—to spread their message. Their rhetoric escalated, with Gnanasara declaring at one rally, "This country still has a Sinhala police, a Sinhala army. After today if a single [Muslim] or some other [minority] touches a Sinhalese . . . it will be their end." Such statements, while alarming to some, resonated with many others who felt economically and culturally threatened.

This rhetoric didn't emerge in a vacuum. Sri Lanka had been torn apart by a twenty-six-year civil war that had only ended in 2009. The war had pitted the government against Tamil separatists who were fighting for an independent state. While often framed as an ethnic conflict, with most Tamils being Hindu and most Sinhalese Buddhist, the war left deep scars and heightened tensions among all of Sri Lanka's diverse communities.

One of Gnanasara's fixations was the halal certification of meat products. He claimed it was another example of Islam's undue influence in Sri Lanka. His anti-halal campaign put such pressure on Muslim leaders that Islamic clerics announced the withdrawal of the labeling system. "We are giving up what is important to us," said Mufti Rizwe, president of the Islamic clergy's senior-most body, in March 2013. "We are making a sacrifice in the interest of peace and harmony."

Most people I met told me that, despite his divisive positions, Gnanasara was all but above the law. Sri Lankan President Gotabaya Rajapaksa, who would later be forced to flee in a helicopter amid mass protests, had appointed the monk to lead a task force charged with making legal amendments that were clearly anti-Muslim. Gnanasara received all the attendant privileges of a politician in South Asia, including armed guards and sycophantic deference. Rauff Hakeem, a member of Parliament and leader of the country's largest Muslim political party, told me, "The yellow robes are untouchable."

When confronted about his actions, the monk once told the press that it was his duty to act against any threat to Buddhism. "Attaining nirvana," he declared, "can wait."

On June 15, 2014, Gnanasara arrived in Aluthgama, a town on the west coast of Sri Lanka, ostensibly to support a monk who had argued with some Muslim youths on a busy road. The young men had already been punished—forced by police to kneel before the offended monk and apologize. The monk had slapped them across the face; the monk's supporters then attacked some Muslim-owned shops.

News of Gnanasara's arrival had spread quickly across his social media feeds, where his already sizable following was growing by the hour. A stage was set, and the media invited. By the time he emerged from his chauffeur-driven car—looking more aggrieved than usual—a crowd of some 7,000 had gathered, many of them robed monks, all eager to hear their guru speak.

Forty minutes away, Fihar was at home, still recovering from the birth of her third child just days earlier. As her older children played hide-and-seek nearby, she nursed the baby and chatted with her husband, Muhammed. Soon, their phones began pinging with WhatsApp messages—clips of Gnanasara's speech. "Enough is enough," he declared, urging the cheering crowd to "fight" the country's minorities. When the speech ended, Buddhist mobs surged through Aluthgama, torching Muslim homes and shops. They came in waves—men and women, some even in monks' saffron robes, according to bystanders. Their intent was clear. Many wore helmets and boots, carried swords or swung Molotov cocktails. "Kill the Muslims!" they shouted.

The violence escalated swiftly, spreading farther and faster. It wasn't long before the mobs reached Fihar's village. She stood at the window, her newborn pressed to her chest, listening to the rising cries as they drew closer. Her body was rigid with fear.

"We phoned the police," Fihar told me. "They said, 'We are coming, we're coming,' but they never did."

Also absent were her Sinhalese neighbors, whose children Fihar had taught for many years. The children would come over to her house every evening and sit at her dinner table to learn Tamil. Sometimes they brought her flowers from their garden. "That day," Fihar said, "they forgot about me." When the mobs reached the gates of her home, Fihar and her family had vanished into the dense jungle. All they took with them was the deed to their house and some gold jewelry.

Over the next several hours, Sri Lanka descended into its worst episode of religious violence in decades. Muslims were beaten in the streets, their shops smashed and looted, their homes engulfed in flames. Even mosques were set ablaze.

Fihar returned with her family the following day. Her house was still standing, but the roof had collapsed, and the walls were black with soot. Still weak from childbirth, she felt her knees give way. It took them a year to rebuild their home, she told me. Not only did she refuse to leave the neighborhood, she still teaches the children of the Sinhalese families who live nearby. When I asked why, she told me that she didn't have a choice. But, she added, rather grimly, neither did they. "They need me to teach them," she said. "And I need them to pay me. We need each other."

Fihar's village was a rural idyll. Tall palm trees rustled and hot pink hibiscus flowers cascaded down whitewashed walls. Crows, magpies, pigeons, and parrots filled the air with their cries. Most Muslim families, like hers, owned their homes and traveled by tuk-tuk or motorcycle. Their ambitions stretched far beyond the village; they prepared their children for work in Dubai and Abu Dhabi, where pay was better, dreams a little more within reach, and most people were Muslim. But it was precisely this drive, this readiness to push beyond the boundaries of tradition, that may have made them targets.

When the violence ended, three people were dead—a small number, given the size of the mobs and the police's failure to intervene over nearly twenty-four hours. One likely reason for the low death toll, said Satkunanathan, the former human rights Commissioner, was that the attackers were driven less by a desire to kill than by "economic envy." "Muslims are very good at business," she told me when we met in Colombo. "They prosper." Sinhalese Buddhists, she explained, "would not be able to hold positions in the trader's association."

This economic dimension adds another layer to Sri Lanka's religious tensions. Unlike in some countries, where religion's role in public life has receded, in Sri Lanka faith remains inextricably linked with politics and commerce. The perception that certain minority communities enjoy outsized economic success has long fueled resentment among segments of the Sinhalese majority—resentment that nationalist rhetoric eagerly exploits. For all the talk of Buddhism being under threat, the mobs had gone after shops, homes, and businesses—stealing, smashing, and setting them alight. Their actions suggested that the violence was indeed about something other than just religion.

The afternoon of my visit to Fihar, I had arranged to meet the family of one of the three men who had been killed in the riots. Mohammed Sahuran was shot dead while trying to protect his grocery store from looters. He was nearing middle age, lightly bearded and round-bellied. He had a wife and three children. His brother-in-law described him as devoted to his family and also to his new motorcycle, which he buffed and polished daily.

At Sahuran's house, I was greeted by a pair of lovebirds in a cage. A cat looked longingly up at the tiny creatures, but before it could act, a plump child in a pink hijab came running out to shoo it away. This was Hajra, nine years old now, but only two months old when she lost her father. A few strands of hair clung to her still-babyish face as she looked shyly up at me.

"Hello," she whispered.

Hello, I replied.

"My birds." She pointed.

They're lovely, I said.

She grinned and fled.

In the living room, I found Sahuran's widow, Nawasiya, surrounded by love—her brother and several friends had gathered to support her. We talked briefly, but didn't get far. At the very first mention of her father, little Hajra started to sob. Her mother gently hushed her, but the girl was overwrought. Tears rolled down her cheeks. Nawasiya pulled her close and rocked her.

Nawasiya's brother took the story forward. When the violence started, the family locked their doors, switched off the lights, and drew the curtains. At around 11:00 p.m., they heard the shouts: "The Sinhalese are coming! The Sinhalese are coming!" Believing the mob wouldn't dare attack a place of worship, the family made a run for their mosque, which was only a few minutes away. After he had ushered his wife and children inside, Sahuran stepped back out to check on his shop.

Not long after, the mob reached the mosque and turned on the Muslim men who had formed a human barricade at its gates. Stones were thrown, and live rounds fired. When it was over, vehicles were smouldering, and shards of glass lay scattered across the ground. Several of the men had been shot—bullets lodged in their legs, torsos, and backs. It was there, among the injured, that Sahuran's family found him—cut down on his way to protect what was his. A single, crimson bloom marked his forehead.

Reached by CNN, Gnanasara said that he was unavailable to comment. Dilanthe Withanage, the chief executive of the monk's anti-Muslim group, told the news channel, "It is true our priest spoke in strong words. He blessed the people after chanting verses. He preached to them to conduct themselves peacefully." The allegations against the BBS, Withanage said, were "an attempt to bring disrespect to Buddhist clergy and Buddhism."

Four months after the attacks, in October 2014, the BBS announced plans to collaborate with India's Rashtriya Swayamsevak Sangh (RSS). The Hindu nationalist group had gained significant influence following the 2014 general elections, during which its political wing, the Bharatiya Janata Party, had secured a decisive victory, bringing the grim-faced Narendra Modi to power as prime minister.

Modi had a long record of anti-Muslim rhetoric and governance. He faced persistent allegations of complicity in the 2002 riots in his home state of Gujarat, which left more than a thousand Muslims dead and displaced tens of thousands. A Human Rights Watch report from that year accused his government and the state police of aiding and abetting the violence. For years, Modi was denied entry to the United States, the United Kingdom, and parts of the European Union due to his alleged role in the carnage. Yet, in Gujarat, he was wildly popular among Hindus, repeatedly reelected as chief minister even as his administration enacted policies that targeted Muslims and confined many to ghettos. The travel bans were lifted only after he became prime minister.

"Discussions are at a high level with the RSS," Gnanasara told reporters in Colombo. Although the BBS was anti-Tamil—and therefore anti-Hindu—the enemies of India's Muslims had found friends in Sri Lanka.

The alliance between the BBS and the RSS marked the expansion of a dangerous narrative. What had started as a local issue was now escalating into something much larger. The shared fear and distrust of Muslims united two groups—one Buddhist and the other Hindu—showing how such ideologies can transcend national and religious divides.

For Sri Lanka, still recovering from a long civil war, this was especially troubling.

Outsiders

Colombo was in the midst of a makeover. The Sri Lankan capital now had air-conditioned malls, restaurants serving high tea, and five-star hotels filled with tourists from Saudi Arabia and China. A ruling party politician invited me—pointedly—to meet him at a hotel bar overlooking the Indian Ocean. Cigarette in one hand, iced drink in the other, he scrutinized me over polarized sunglasses and declared that Sri Lanka was perfectly fine. The events that had brought me there suggested otherwise. I had come to trace the fault lines: to meet militant monks, listen to survivors, and speak with those trying, in different ways, to hold the country together. My journey began in Colombo, but I spent most of my time in two towns scarred by violence—Aluthgama and Digana, attacked in 2014 and 2018, respectively.

I was accompanied on my travels by S. N. Ganeshan, an ethnic Tamil who spoke fluent Tamil, Sinhalese, and English. Nayan, as he asked to be called, identified as an "Up-Country Tamil," a descendant of South Indians whom the British relocated across the Palk Strait in the nineteenth and twentieth centuries to labor on tea plantations. This group was considered distinct from the country's indigenous Tamil community, the Ceylon Tamils, who traced their ancestry to the island's ancient Tamil kingdoms and have lived in Sri Lanka for over a thousand years.

I hadn't asked Nayan for this information, and I wasn't the only one with whom he shared it over the next few days. When he didn't bring it up, some of the people we were interviewing asked outright: Was he Tamil? If so, where from? Only then did I realize that Nayan—a soft-spoken, gentle giant of a man—was offering people exactly what they needed to decide how to relate to him. Viewed in the context of the island's history, this need to situate anyone not obviously Sinhalese in an ethnic, religious, and historical framework was yet another indication that Sri Lanka was perhaps not fine.

I first visited Sri Lanka in the early 2000s, during the final years of the civil war. I landed in Colombo, the Sinhalese Buddhist-dominated capital, where an immigration officer encouraged me to enjoy my stay before urging me to avoid the north, where the minority Hindu Tamils lived. After a couple of restless days in leafy, low-key Colombo, I found myself unable to follow his advice. The slow-moving city felt trapped in a dream.

By then, the north of Sri Lanka was largely under the control of the Liberation Tigers of Tamil Eelam (LTTE), the armed separatist group formed in 1976 in response to decades of state-led discrimination against Tamils. When I visited, only the Jaffna Peninsula remained outside LTTE control—retaken by the Sri Lankan military. Life in Jaffna felt brittle. Men in lungis and women in tightly wrapped saris, children in tow, moved with a palpable urgency, as if eager to reach home and bolt the doors behind them. Sinhalese soldiers patrolled with rifles raised—even pointing them at children. Children were among the tens of thousands who had vanished from homes, schools, and checkpoints. The names of the missing, like the stories of rape, torture, and mass graves, traveled in half-uttered fragments, as if speaking of them might summon the same fate. The people lived each day balanced between silence and survival.

The Tamils I spoke to despised the Sri Lankan army and government and yearned for a country of their own. Not all agreed with the LTTE's tactics—suicide bombings, the recruitment of children as soldiers—but they called the LTTE "our boys" and described them as heroes and legends. Meanwhile, most of the Sinhalese I met wanted the LTTE crushed by any means necessary. They were frustrated with the government's inability to defeat the group, despite military aid from India and Israel and Western powers' widespread condemnation of the insurgents.

One might have expected the Buddhist clergy to play a pacifying role. Instead, many high-profile monks pushed for intensified military action, leading the local media to coin the term "war monks." Among them was Athuraliye Rathana Thero, a leading figure in the creation of the Jathika Hela Urumaya (JHU), or the National Heritage Party, which Gnanasara would later join. The JHU is widely viewed as the mother ship of modern Buddhist nationalism, fostering anti-minority sentiment in Sri Lanka much as the RSS had in India. "Talk can come later," Rathana told *The* (UK) *Telegraph* in 2007. "We need war." Today, he is a four-time member of Parliament who continues to deliver inflammatory speeches and stages hunger strikes to push his agenda.

Founded in 2004, the JHU won nine seats in the general elections that year. For the first time, Buddhist monks sat in Parliament alongside career politicians. The party's "greatest concern," noted Iselin Frydenlund, a professor of Religious Studies at the MF Norwegian School of Theology, Religion and Society was that peace talks would give the LTTE what it was fighting for. "The majority of the Buddhist monks perceived this not only as a threat to the physical integrity of the state," Frydenlund writes, "but in fact also to Buddhism itself."

The war lasted twenty-six years, claiming between 80,000 and 100,000 lives. Many others—mostly Tamils—remain unaccounted for. In May 2009, President Mahinda Rajapaksa delivered his victory speech at the Temple of the Tooth, Sri Lanka's most sacred Buddhist shrine. At the telling choice of venue he vowed to never permit the "bifurcation of the Motherland." The government's victory over the LTTE "turned the country into a Sinhala and Buddhist euphoria," observed Frydenlund, "in which political Buddhist movements such as the JHU, or its newer—and far more violent—offshoot the Bodu Bala Sena, enjoy even more fertile grounds for them to prosper."

After the war, Sinhalese nationalists were left without a cause. Sri Lanka is a country that "always needs an enemy," said Shihar Aneez, a journalist who spent twelve years covering the island's politics and economy for Reuters. "When you don't have an enemy, people are going to question you," he told me one afternoon in a Colombo coffee shop. "You need an enemy so that people don't focus on 'unnecessary' issues."

With the backing of Sinhalese nationalist politicians like the Rajapaksas, militant monks turned their gaze toward Sri Lanka's Muslims, casting them as outsiders whose religious and cultural practices posed an existential threat to Sinhala-Buddhist identity—just as they had once claimed of the Tamils. Yet

Muslims had long been woven into the island's fabric. Arriving as Arab traders in the seventh century, they had built deep-rooted communities, and were as integral to Sri Lanka's identity as any other religious group. But for nationalists eager to consolidate power—where fear translated into political capital—Muslims served a different function. By portraying them as aligned with a global Islamic order rather than the Sri Lankan state, nationalists suggested they could never truly belong. In doing so, groups like the Bodu Bala Sena helped stoke a moral panic, recasting Muslims as the ultimate "other."

Although the mob attack on Fihar's village was one of the most prominent episodes of anti-Muslim violence in Sri Lanka, it was far from unique. Between 2012 and 2015, according to state agencies and human rights groups, Muslims were targeted in hundreds of incidents. This wave of hostility mirrored a broader surge of Islamophobia worldwide—one that had been gathering force since 9/11 and hardened with the rise of the Islamic State. In June 2014, Abu Bakr al-Baghdadi declared the creation of a caliphate across Syria and Iraq. That same year, Modi rose to power in India, carried by a tide of nationalism that cast minorities, especially Muslims, as enemies within.

This narrative sat uneasily beside the Buddhist ideal of ahimsa, or non-harming. Monks are meant to embody this principle. Yet in Sri Lanka, where religion and politics were tightly entwined, moments of crisis often peeled back the veneer of peace, revealing an instinct for aggression. The militant monks who stoked anti-Muslim hatred were not outliers—they were expressions of how completely Buddhism had been conscripted to serve the ambitions of the state. By the time I returned to Sri Lanka, more than a decade after the civil war ended, a new set of divisions had taken hold. The violence now was different—targeted, contained. It no longer resembled a single conflagration, but a series of smaller, smoldering fires, each capable of flaring out of control.

Sometimes, between interviews, I would stop at Buddhist temples and shrines. You didn't need to be religious to feel moved by the rituals: lighting incense, offering fresh flowers, turning a prayer wheel. Though I couldn't follow the mantras, I felt the peace they invoked. In moments like those, I struggled to reconcile Buddhism's promise of compassion with the hostility unfolding around me.

As a Catholic, I've wrestled all my life with the stain of complicity within my own faith. In Europe, many churches stand tall not only as monuments to devotion, but to empires built on the backs of enslaved people and stolen lands in the Americas, Asia, and Africa. Marble pillars and gilded altars were often paid for with blood money. Those reminders were never far from my mind in Sri Lanka where I found myself returning to a familiar question: Are Buddhist monks so different from priests and clerics who vow to serve a higher purpose, yet sometimes lose their way? They are expected to be better than everyone else. But in a world shaped by conflict and fear, perhaps no vow—no matter how sacred—is entirely safe from the pull of politics.

"Sinhalese-Buddhist Entitlement Complex"

In *In Defense of Dharma,* the scholar Tessa Bartholomeusz challenges the popular belief that nonviolence in Buddhism is absolute, arguing that while it is a core principle, it is not without exceptions. "Some Buddhists asserted that, though a Buddhist king should be committed to non-violence, he might be called upon to cancel his commitment under certain conditions. Such is his duty and . . . such is his karma—to engage in violence and war."

Several Sri Lankan monks Bartholomeusz met during her travels—including in the civil war years—invoked a similar rationale to justify their embrace of violence. Their defense rested on a story from Buddhist mythology. In the time of the Buddha, two kings—Ajatasattu and Pasenadi—were locked in a fight for supremacy that Ajatasattu ultimately won. "The Buddha assesses the character of the two kings: King Ajatasattu, who initiates the attacks, emerges as the king who is 'a friend of evil (papa), an acquaintance of evil, intimate with evil.' On the other hand, King Pasenadi, even though he also armed himself, is considered by the Buddha to be 'a friend of virtue (kalyana), an acquaintance of virtue, intimate with virtue,'" Bartholomeusz writes.

In defending himself against Ajatasattu's assault, Pasenadi is not seen as unethical, but as virtuous. The message, according to the monks the scholar interviewed, is that morality in war is not determined solely by the act of violence—but by the intent behind it.

The Buddhist monks I spoke with offered a different perspective, grounded in the *Mahavamsa*, or Great Chronicle, a sixth-century court document that recounts the arrival of Buddhism in Sri Lanka. According to this text, Buddhism reached the island through the efforts of King Ashoka of the Mauryan Empire, which extended across the Indian subcontinent. A devoted convert to Buddhism, Ashoka sought not only to strengthen the faith within India but also to spread it abroad. The *Mahavamsa* recounts how he sent his children to Sri Lanka with a cutting of the Bodhi tree under which the Buddha had attained enlightenment, along with precious relics, including the Buddha's rice bowl and collarbone. In a message to the ruler of Sri Lanka, Ashoka urged: "Take refuge in the Buddha, as I have taken refuge in the Buddha." In 250 BCE, the Sri Lankan king converted to Buddhism at a royal park, which he then dedicated as the site of a monastery and an enormous stupa to house the sacred relics.

Another key episode in the *Mahavamsa* ties Sri Lanka's destiny to a figure named Vijaya, who, according to legend, landed on the island on the day of the Buddha's death. Every Buddhist country has its own myth about how it came under the Buddha's spell—or was chosen by him. This was Sri Lanka's. The chronicle recounts that the Buddha, aware of Vijaya's arrival, declared: "Vijaya, son of King Sihabahu, [has] come to Lanka from the country of Lala, together with seven hundred followers. In Lanka, O lord of gods, will my religion be established; therefore, carefully protect him with his followers and Lanka."

According to the text, "Sri Lanka is the Dharmadvipa (the island of the faith) consecrated by the Buddha himself as the land in which his teachings would flourish," notes Sri Lankan scholar Nira Wickramasinghe. According to this common interpretation, Sri Lanka is not only a Buddhist nation but one under divine protection, with Sinhalese Buddhists chosen by the Buddha himself to uphold the faith. This narrative reinforces the notion that the Sinhalese people have a historical destiny not just to rule Sri Lanka, but to save, at all costs, Buddhism itself. Gehan Gunatilleke, a lawyer and Oxford academic, identifies this episode from the *Mahavamsa* as having laid the foundation of what he calls the "Sinhala-Buddhist entitlement complex." He writes that the myth is now viewed by most Sri Lankans as "indisputable history."

The hero of the *Mahavamsa* was King Dutthagamani, who waged war against the Hindu Tamils for control of the island in 165 BCE. The battle ended only when Dutthagamani drove a spear through his Tamil rival, King Elara. But as he surveyed the carnage around him, Dutthagamani found no joy, even though he had secured absolute power for the Sinhalese. All he could think about were the lives he had taken. Fearing that their king might lose his killer's resolve, a group of monks reassured him: Far from having slaughtered scores, they told him, he had killed only "one and a half human beings."

In their view, a true human being was someone who had embraced Buddhism by accepting the Buddha, his teachings (Dharma), and his community (monks and nuns)—in essence, a practicing Buddhist. Those who adhered to certain aspects of the Buddha's teachings without fully committing to them were regarded as "half-human." Most of the king's victims, however, were Hindus, and the monks argued that this rendered them "not more to be esteemed than beasts."

The rhetoric used to dehumanize outsiders in Sri Lanka—once Hindus, now Muslims and Christians—has long been visceral, menacing, and politically expedient. This approach is neither new nor isolated; throughout history, similar language has justified occupation, enslavement, and genocide, from the British Empire's colonial rule to the Islamic State's massacres. In liberal democracies, this logic has found new champions. Donald Trump compared undocumented immigrants to pests, describing them as an "infestation." Modi likened Muslims to stray dogs, while his Bharatiya Janata Party colleagues called them "termites." In October 2023, while announcing a total siege on Gaza, Israeli Defense Minister Yoav Gallant called Palestinians "human animals." As the novelist Omar El Akkad observes, reflecting on how language is used to justify violence: "When those dying are deemed human enough to warrant discussion, discussion must be had. When they're deemed nonhuman, discussion becomes offensive, an affront to civility."

Casting human beings as vermin to be exterminated or animals to be caged normalizes the idea that one group can annihilate another without consequence. After all, if a victim is no longer seen as human, are they even a victim?

To understand how such narratives have taken root in Sri Lanka, we must look to its colonial past—when religion and power became tightly entwined. When British forces arrived at the Port of Colombo in 1815 and wrested control from the Dutch, who had displaced the Portuguese, Buddhism was so deeply enmeshed with the state that kings needed the monks' endorsement to rule unchallenged. In return, the clergy received royal patronage: land grants, cash, and subsidies. Upon defeating the Kingdom of Kandy and securing the island, the British pledged to protect Buddhism as a strategy to maintain stability. But as the empire expanded, Christian missionaries arrived in growing numbers under the banner of "Christianity, commerce, and civilization." They built churches, Sunday schools, and youth groups, spreading their belief in the superiority of their religion and race.

As it became clear the British had no intention of honoring their promise, Buddhist monks across Ceylon began to regroup. This marked a new era of organized resistance. Clergy established ecclesiastical colleges, revived print culture, and publicly debated rival faiths. In 1873, in the coastal town of Panadura, Buddhist monks challenged Christian missionaries in a two-day public debate. The event sparked a national stir—and drew international attention.

Among those captivated by the encounter was Henry Steel Olcott, a former U.S. Army colonel who had cofounded the Theosophical Society with Helena Blavatsky, a spiritual medium and self-styled thaumaturge. Olcott knew little about Buddhism. But when he arrived in Colombo in May of 1880, dressed in a rumpled white suit and wire-rimmed spectacles, his beard cascading like a waterfall, he and Blavatsky received a royal welcome. "A huge crowd awaited us," he later recalled, "and rent the air with their united shout of 'Sadhu! Sadhu!' A white cloth was spread for us from the jetty steps to the road where carriages were ready, and a thousand flags were frantically waved in welcome."

Olcott had the appearance of a wandering prophet, and he was immediately cast in the role of the anti-missionary. "America of course appeared in those days as the great anticolonialist Western power, the successful rebel against British rule," Richard Gombrich and Gananath Obeyesekere explain. "So Olcott was welcomed as a political and cultural ally who could assist the Sinhalas in their struggle and also bring to bear the organizational skills of the West."

Olcott moved swiftly. He founded the Buddhist Theosophical Society, designed a Buddhist flag, and compiled a catechism. He lobbied the colonial government to declare Vesak, which commemorates the Buddha's birth, enlightenment, and death, a public holiday, and encouraged Buddhists to mark it with Christmas-style carols and greeting cards. His efforts, argues Sri Lankan linguist Macbool Alimmohamed Nuhman, marked "the beginning of Sinhala Buddhist nationalism."

Olcott's most famous protégé was Don David Hewavitharana, who was born in Ceylon in 1864. Hewavitharana belonged to a wealthy family of furniture entrepreneurs who sent him to Christian missionary schools to learn English and study a Western curriculum. The plan backfired, for the boy was bullied by his fellow students and developed a strong dislike for his teachers. The Christian clergymen disgusted their student with their fondness for meat, alcohol, and hunting. Hewavitharana left school for a clerical position in the colonial education department; at eighteen, he quit that job to work as an interpreter for Olcott. Hewavitharana's association with the theosophists took him beyond the shores of the little island, giving him exactly the sort of exposure his parents had wished to avoid. He went to India and Japan and studied Pali, the language of the Buddhist scriptures. In 1881, Don David assumed the name Anagarika Dharmapala. Dharmapala means "defender of the faith," and, like many who discover religion later in life, he exuded the zeal and vigor of a new convert. Although he still let his hair grow, he was celibate, and dressed only in yellow robes.

In 1893, Dharmapala attended the historic World Parliament of Religions in Chicago. To its Christian organizers, their faith was the great "universal religion." But Dharmapala pointed instead to the Buddha, who had preached compassion and truth centuries before Christ. He spoke of tolerance and gentleness—not as abstract ideals but as Buddhist principles urgently needed in an increasingly fractured world. The audience, rapt, seemed to agree. Just days later, Dharmapala presided over another historic moment. At a meeting of the Theosophical Society in Chicago, Charles T. Strauss, a New York businessman, took vows to become a Buddhist—reportedly the first American to do so. The act carried the weight of a new beginning.

Half a world away, such spiritual awakenings were increasingly becoming a rallying cry against colonial oppression. In India, the Khilafat Movement—launched by Indian Muslims to protest British policies toward the Ottoman Empire—merged anti-colonial sentiments with religious fervor. The movement emphasized that political sovereignty was inseparable from religious sovereignty, and vice versa. Central to the Khilafat Movement was the defense of Islam. While the Khilafat campaign fostered cross-religious solidarity, particularly through its alliance with Gandhi's Non-Cooperation Movement, among more extremist factions, it provoked fear. One such group was the Arya Samaj, an influential ideological precursor to the Hindu nationalist Rashtriya Swayamsevak Sangh.

The 1921 colonial census became a flash point, Sana Aiyar, historian of Modern South Asia at MIT, told me. It reported that while Muslims remained a minority in India, their population was growing at a faster rate than Hindus and Buddhists. In 1926, Arya Samaj leader Swami Shraddhananda published *Hindu Sangathan: Saviour of the Dying Race*, warning of an existential crisis for Hindus. He called for unity and sought to prevent lower-caste conversions to other religions.

In an effort to forge cultural links with other Asian countries, and establish India as a civilizational anchor, the Arya Samaj cast Buddhism as a shared spiritual legacy—one that had spread from India to Tibet, China, Ceylon, and Burma, and from China to Korea and Japan. They saw Buddhism as having deeply influenced the spiritual and moral lives of people across the continent, much in the way Christianity had shaped the West. This framing raised an uncomfortable question: If Buddhism had such a powerful impact elsewhere, why had it faded in the land where it was born? The Arya Samaj blamed its decline mainly on the arrival of Islam—a view that many historians dispute. Still, it was a narrative that appealed to figures like Dharmapala, who was drawn to Hindu reform movements. The ideological positions developed by both Buddhist and Hindu leaders—in response to colonial domination—would go on to complicate the building of inclusive democracies in the postcolonial era.

At the same time, religious syncretism and cultural exchange were widespread. Many decades later, in the 1980s, historians Gombrich and Obeysekera documented that a Kali shrine, typically associated with Hindu worship, was frequented by Sinhalese Buddhists from all walks of life, ranging from affluent individuals arriving in Mercedes-Benzes to those who were clearly indigent. They also observed that Tamil Hindus, particularly in the northern and eastern regions of the island, revered important Buddhist pilgrimage sites, often participating in festivals or visiting sacred spaces acknowledged by both traditions.

But even as Buddhist and Hindu traditions mingled, the political divide between Sinhalese Buddhists and Tamil Hindus widened. While Dharmapala was stirring things up, Ceylon Tamils were climbing the colonial ladder. They learned English, secured civil service jobs, and came to be seen as favorites of the British. When the British withdrew in 1948, a baseless rumor began to circulate: that a Tamil takeover was imminent, backed by Tamils from across the strait in India. The claim had no basis in fact, but it stoked paranoia among the Sinhalese majority.

Solomon Bandaranaike, an ambitious Sri Lankan politician, capitalized on this fear during his 1956 campaign for prime minister, promising to make Sinhala the island's sole official language. Sinhala wasn't even Bandaranaike's strength—his fluency lay in English, polished during his years as a student at Oxford and as a barrister in London. Once in office, on what happened to be the 2,500th anniversary of the Buddha's attainment of Nirvana, he kept his word by signing the Official Language Act, which excluded many Tamils from government positions.

In *Brotherless Night*, V. V. Ganeshananthan, a Tamil of Sri Lankan descent, captures the shift through her narrator's memory: "The majority Sinhalese, smarting at slights perceived and actual, discovered ways for the country to promote their Buddha, their language, and their histories—a comeuppance for us, for Tamils, who were a minority, and who had flourished in English. Learn Sinhalese, or leave your job, Tamil civil servants were told—my father among them. I still haven't forgotten the look on his face when he told us . . . I could not say a word in Sinhala. My future depended on a language I did not know, no one wanted to teach me, and, on principle, I did not want to learn."

Despite this, Tamils continued to prosper in business, further inflaming Sinhalese nationalists. Anti-Tamil violence followed in 1956, 1958, 1977, 1981, and 1983. The 1983 pogrom, known as "Black July," saw widespread attacks on Tamils, with thousands displaced, and marked the beginning of the civil war. Prime Minister Bandaranaike later attempted to reverse his "Sinhala Only" policy by signing an agreement that offered limited autonomy to Tamil-majority regions. But under pressure from hardline nationalists, he publicly tore up the agreement, effectively nullifying it. By then, however, the damage was done.

One Friday in September 1959, the sixty-year-old prime minister was receiving petitioners in his residence when a young Buddhist monk approached him. As Bandaranaike bowed respectfully, the monk drew a .45 caliber revolver from his robes and fired two shots at close range. Staggering back into the foyer, Bandaranaike was struck a third time, before succumbing to his wounds. His killing marked a grim turning point: Monks had moved beyond shaping ideology—they were now enforcing it. The robe had taken up the sword.

“We Never Use Violence”

Three months after the 2014 mob attack in Aluthgama, the monk Galagoda Aththe Gnanasara hosted a special guest in Sri Lanka: Ashin Wirathu, a Burmese monk who had founded the 969 movement and the Ma Ba Tha organization. The two monks shared an obsession with Muslim men. Wirathu propagated a theory he called “the sex strategy,” which alleged that Muslim men were seducing Burmese women in a bid to overtake Myanmar’s Buddhist population and turn the country into an Islamic state.

At the time of his visit, Wirathu was already the world’s most notorious Buddhist monk. In 2013, he had appeared on the cover of *Time* magazine with the headline “The Face of Buddhist Terror,” highlighting his role in inciting deadly riots in towns like Meiktila, where dozens of Muslims were killed. Despite this, the Sri Lankan government not only approved his visa but also gave him a security detail. At a stadium packed with tens of thousands of monks, nuns, and laypeople eager to hear him speak, Wirathu announced that his 969 movement would collaborate with Gnanasara's Bodu Bala Sena to "protect Buddhism around the world." He offered no further clarification, leaving his message open to interpretation. "It's the responsibility of monks, as Buddha's sons, to teach bad and uncivilized people to become good and civilized," he said.

The rally marked a major success for Gnanasara, boosting his profile among Sri Lanka's growing rabble of militant monks. With his rising influence, his speeches became increasingly inflammatory. He expressed disdain for women in hijab and made false claims about the Quran allowing Muslims to acquire the wealth of non-Muslims through fraudulent means. When Muslim leaders challenged his fabrications, he issued the chilling threat of "another Aluthgama."

That threat materialized after a group of Muslim men assaulted a Sinhalese Buddhist truck driver in late February 2018, in Digana, a small town in Sri Lanka's Central Province. When the driver died from his injuries, mainstream media and social networks amplified the story, with posts on Facebook and WhatsApp calling for revenge. One widely shared post quoted a monk telling his followers: "The sword at home is no longer for cutting jackfruit—sharpen it and go."

Among the militant monks, Sinhalese nationalists, and angry young men who converged on Digana was Ampitiye Sumanarathana Thero, a notorious social media personality and ordained monk from Batticaloa, a city on the island's eastern coast. Sumanarathana enjoyed filming himself threatening minorities. In one viral video, he marched up to a man until he stood so close their noses nearly touched. His hands emerged from the folds of his robe like claws and he bellowed, spit flying from his mouth: "Every single Tamil will be cut into pieces! They will all be killed! All the Tamils in the south will be butchered! The Sinhalese will massacre them." In another widely circulated clip, shared with his hundreds of thousands of Facebook followers, he slapped a Christian clergyman whom he accused of missionary activities in a Buddhist area.

In Digana, Sumanarathana stormed into a police station to demand the arrest of the Muslims involved in the assault on the truck driver.

Gnanasara also came to town, ostensibly to offer condolences to the dead man's family. Within hours of his arrival, a Muslim-owned grocery store was looted and set on fire. Later, a mob of several hundred descended with sticks, stones, and gasoline. Worshippers at a local mosque fled into the surrounding snake-infested jungles. They later recounted how the mob entered the mosque grounds, poured kerosene on motorbikes, and desecrated copies of the Quran. "The mosque was destroyed," an onlooker told me. "We had to rebuild it from scratch."

Families returned to a ruined landscape. Garden hoses were all they had to extinguish the remaining flames.

During this chaos the body of twenty-seven-year-old Abdul Basith was discovered. Basith's parents operated a shop out of their two-story home. When the mob set the building ablaze, Basith, who had recently started a job as a journalist, became trapped on the second floor. His brother later testified before a fact-finding committee that police officers stood by and did nothing to extinguish the flames.

The final toll was devastating: over three hundred homes, more than two hundred shops, dozens of vehicles, twenty mosques, two Hindu temples—and Abdul Basith was dead. "The state failed in its duty to protect the Muslim minority during attacks; hold perpetrators to account; and deliver justice," declared Amnesty International. The international outcry finally prompted action. The government arrested more than a hundred people, including prominent Sinhalese nationalist leaders. Yet, despite their key roles in inciting the violence, the monks Sumanarathana and Gnanasara remained untouched by the law.

I arrived in Digana in the summer of 2023 to meet Mohamad Hamud, a man whose reckless decisions had led to the death of the truck driver—an act that set off a chain reaction, igniting tensions that would engulf his town in flames. We met at a mosque, which, like nearly every house on the street, had been looted and torched. On a gatepost, a small mailbox labeled "Police Record Box" hung crookedly.

A worshipper told me that the police were now supposed to patrol the area and log their observations in the book inside. Five years had passed since the attacks, and, according to him, the police needed repeated reminders to appear. "We tread on water," he said. "At any moment, a huge wave could swallow us whole." Then, after a pause, he added, "These days, when there's an accident in the village, the first thing we ask is: Who is he? Is he Muslim, is he Tamil, or is he Buddhist?"

We passed newly planted trees and climbed the steps into the mosque, where a group of men sat on chairs in a circle. The windows were open, and a breeze stirred the room. After introducing myself, I asked what they remembered. One man described hiding in a drainpipe during the riots. Another said he could still smell the gasoline. "We couldn't save a spoon," murmured a third. Then Hamud entered, and the room fell silent. A few men nodded in acknowledgment, their expressions wary; others looked openly hostile. Unfazed, Hamud walked over to the only other young man in the room. He winked and whispered something into his friend's ear, prompting a strained laugh.

As the conversation resumed, the men began to list what they had lost—cars, orchards, vegetable gardens, bakeries, furniture showrooms. As the list grew, Hamud's confidence began to unravel. "I didn't do anything," he said suddenly, his voice catching. "My friends may have done it, but not me."

That Thursday in February 2018, Hamud had invited three friends over. They planned to attend a wedding later that night, and Hamud wanted to start the celebrations early. He was twenty-seven, a tuk-tuk driver of six years. When business was slow, he picked up odd jobs—house painting, plastering. That night, he drank. Sometime after midnight, the four men piled into a tuk-tuk, with Hamud at the wheel. When a truck overtook them, clipping the tuk-tuk's side mirror, Hamud's friends urged him to give chase. The truck eventually stopped at a petrol station. Hamud recounted that a "small argument" broke out and that his "friends tried to fight" the driver. The confrontation escalated quickly, a local newspaper reported. All four men allegedly attacked the lorry driver with iron rods, beating him until he collapsed. Afterward, they went into hiding, reemerging only when police announced that arrests were imminent.

Now thirty-two, Hamud looked worn down by his own telling. His ribs and limbs jutted like scaffolding. His eyes were jaundiced. His jeans sagged on his thin frame. He had spent nine and a half months in jail and was out on bail, but the trial dragged on—another sentence in slow motion. Closure, if it came, was still far off. The men kept talking. Hamud said nothing. When I looked at his chair a moment later, he was gone.

Gnanasara kept me waiting for days before he finally agreed to meet me just hours before I was due to leave Colombo. When the time came, his armed guard led me into a dim room that reeked of stale incense. The militant monk sat at the far end, hunched over his phone.

He was fatter than I had expected, and his robe kept slipping off his shoulder, exposing loose, pale flesh. He didn't bother fixing it. A group of monks in neon orange robes filed in behind me, smiling blandly. One of them started lecturing me about Buddhism. "You have to practice it," he droned. "Don't do bad things." Gnanasara finally looked up, scowling. "Enough," he barked. His spokesman, Dilanthe Withanage, translated with an apologetic smile.

Withanage was an odd character. Armed with an electronics engineering degree from Tbilisi, Georgia, he dedicated his time in Sri Lanka to defending Gnanasara's hate speech. In an interview with a news magazine, he had accused Christian evangelicals of luring Buddhists to convert with promises of material reward. "They come, they preach, they tarnish the image of Buddhism here," he said. "And they offer jobs, they offer positions, if they convert to Christianity. And jobs are offered, houses are offered."

During my time on the island, I noticed a shift: The hostility once directed at Muslims was now turning toward Christians. Newspapers carried reports of pastors attacked, churches vandalized, and worship obstructed. It was as if the monks had decided they had taken their campaign against Muslims as far as it could go—and now needed a new enemy to remain relevant and keep their audience engaged. The U.S. Department of State's 2023 report on international religious freedom documented forty-three incidents of violence and intimidation against

Christians in Sri Lanka. According to the National Christian Evangelical Alliance of Sri Lanka, many of these attacks were carried out by Buddhist groups, often led by monks. The pattern made something plain: Militant monks were not acting out of spontaneous fervor, but with strategy—and political calculation.

I asked if Gnanasara saw himself as a political leader. Withanage translated with a beaming smile, as though he knew the question would flatter.

"That's how people choose to see me," the monk said with a smirk, before slipping into a well-worn tirade about the need to defend Buddhism from foreign contamination. He waddled toward a plush armchair, tucking his phone into his robe; each notification lit up his belly like a lantern. "We must protect our culture," he declared. "But we never use violence."

Who exactly was he protecting it from, I asked. He didn't hesitate. The Easter bombings. He pointed to the 2019 attacks on churches and luxury hotels—carried out by domestic Muslim extremists—as proof of what he called a broader Muslim conspiracy to destabilize the country. He alluded grimly to an "organized network" operating in the shadows.

When I suggested his own rhetoric might fuel violence, he snorted.

"The media twists everything," he said. "They even claimed I threatened to slice up a Muslim politician. How could I say such a thing?" He broke into loud laughter. The monks around him followed instantly, their laughter swelling until the room rang with it—as if it were all just a joke. They sipped tea and chewed cashew nuts—urging me to help myself—and turned their attention back to their phones, scrolling casually.

Withanage, engineer and ideologue, continued to translate Gnanasara's staccato Sinhalese. The monk's historical revisionism painted a picture of a Ceylon united by Buddhism until the British arrived with their divisive Christianity. Now, Gnanasara declared, the BBS was on a crusade to rectify this colonial meddling. As our conversation unfolded, Gnanasara's demeanor oscillated between smug self-satisfaction and barely contained aggression. He spoke of "fighting" for Buddhist values with unsettling frequency, all the while insisting on the BBS's commitment to nonviolence.

As I left, Gnanasara tried to soften things. "We may have made mistakes," he admitted, walking me to the door. Then, grinning like a wolf: "But we always serve tea to visitors."

Part Two

Myanmar

Abbot Zero

The Moei River carves a fragile boundary between Thailand's Mae Sot district and Myanmar's Myawaddy town, a watery seam where refugees fleeing the war-torn country risk everything. Some pay human traffickers to guide them; others slip through on moonless nights on low, quiet boats. A lucky few—those with "clean" passports that don't mark them as dissenters—walk over the bridge, carrying whatever they can: doddering parents, dogs and cats and chickens, bundles of clothing and boom boxes.

Since the military coup in February 2021 and the ensuing civil war, tens of thousands have fled Myanmar, joining the millions already displaced by decades of religious, ethnic, and authoritarian persecution. So many people have poured across this dingy little waterway that this nondescript town on Thailand's western edge now feels as much Burmese as Thai. Tea shops serve Burmese breakfast noodles in fish broth and young men fleeing the military conscription imposed by the junta in 2024 hustle along the roadside selling counterfeit Johnnie Walker whiskey, condoms, and cigarettes. They use the proceeds to pay off Thai police tasked with hunting down illegal immigrants.

Mae Sot is more than a refuge for displaced souls—it is a crucible where exiled politicians, tech innovators building systems to document human rights abuses, resistance fighters, and Buddhist monks converge. All have fled Myanmar and sought sanctuary in Thailand, yet, the border traffic flows both ways. Chinese visitors frequently cross over to Myawaddy, a town notorious for its casinos and rampant trade in alcohol and drugs. Equally infamous are its scam centers, run by Chinese warlords on Burmese militia-owned land. The warlords lure workers under false pretenses to dupe victims worldwide out of tens of billions of dollars through crypto fraud and fake investment schemes. By day, the sky radiates a crystalline blue, banana trees sway, scarecrows in collared shirts guard the paddy, and wandering goats kick at the town's dusty earth. By night, explosions from across the Burmese border punctuate the darkness.

I had come to Mae Sot to meet a monk on the run from another monk. The man I sought was known as Abbot Zero. That was not his real name but an "activist" moniker he adopted to protect himself from the junta that had included his real name on their ever-growing list of dissenters—people who risk jail, or worse, if caught. Abbot Zero was the protégé of Ashin Wirathu, one of modern Buddhism's most polarizing figures, and the very man from whom Zero now needed protection. Wirathu, who ten years earlier had announced a partnership with Sri Lankan extremists to "protect Buddhists worldwide," didn't much care for the fact that the younger monk, who knew so many of his secrets, had chosen a different path.

Widely seen as a driving force behind Myanmar's surge of anti-Muslim hatred, Wirathu helped fuel the genocide in Rakhine State in 2016 and 2017. I'd heard endless accounts of him while traveling in Sri Lanka, yet my attempts to meet him were thwarted. Word was that he remained at his temple in Mandalay, Myanmar's second-largest city—a place where legal entry for journalists was nearly impossible. The junta had made sure of that.

Formally known as the Tatmadaw, the junta wields immense power in Myanmar. Its role is not unlike that of the British colonizers whose interventions in the country at the end of the 1800s laid the ground for the merciless nationalism that has since come to define it. The junta commands the military, police, and security forces, who are heavily armed with weapons from Russia and China. It controls people: Protesters are shot dead, dissidents are jailed, and genocidal attacks on the Rohingya are meticulously orchestrated. The junta dominates the economy, profiting from the export of teak, jade, hydrocarbons, and emeralds, while remaining deeply entrenched in illicit industries such as narcotics, human and wildlife trafficking, smuggling, and sex work. And, as I discovered in Mae Sot, the junta's reach extends even to some of the country's most revered figures: Buddhist monks.

Since the coup, the exiled opposition had only swelled. There were more dissidents with public profiles outside Myanmar than within it, and Mae Sot had emerged as one of their most vital hubs. Here, hopeful Burmese clung to the words of Pablo Neruda, once painted on walls across their homeland: "You can cut all the flowers, but you can't stop spring from coming." Chief among these revolutionaries was Abbot Zero.

In the spring of 2024, I flew from London to Bangkok, then caught a provincial flight to Mae Sot. The cabin was packed with young people—Thai teenagers returning from shopping trips in the capital, dressed in oversized sweatshirts and hauling carry-ons stuffed with unopened sneaker boxes, alongside young Burmese, identifiable by their language. Many, I gathered, were traveling to Mae Sot to see relatives, perhaps even to slip across the river for a brief, albeit dangerous, visit home. The plane buzzed with conversation, filling the space with a restless energy. Flight attendants moved through the aisle with cups of tea, maintaining order in a crowd bound by youth yet divided by fate.

Watching them, I was reminded of how decades of military rule had shaped—and constricted—the prospects of Burmese youth. Following the latest coup, another generation had now been forced into exile. For the rest of the world, the crisis in Myanmar had receded into the background—one among many mushrooming across the globe. But for the young passengers on that plane, the journey was very much ongoing.

This sense of loss was not new to Myanmar whose modern struggles echoed an earlier era, when foreign powers altered the course of its history.

The British captured Burma in 1886, and the country was thereafter administered as a province of British India. The occupation sparked immediate fears of religious and cultural extinction. "Panic reigns over Mandalay. The country is completely ravaged. The Burmese do not at all want annexation," a Rangoon local confided in a visiting Russian Indologist that year. "They are afraid of the British; they are afraid of the violence and annihilation of their faith. The monks dread particularly the fate of Buddhism."

As in nearby geographies colonized by the British in this period, including Ceylon and India, the occupation of Burma served as a rallying cry. Burmese Buddhists organized programs for religious reform, founded schools, and published journals. To emphasize their commitment, they curtailed spending on lavish temple rituals. Prompted by the hope that a "renewed enthusiasm and devotion" could counter the erosion of the Buddha's teachings, the besieged Buddhists came together with "a sense of common purpose and belonging," observed the scholar Alicia Turner in her book *Saving Buddhism: The Impermanence of Religion in Colonial Burma.*

The country teemed with foreign religious influences vying for a foothold—from orthodox Christian missionaries to reformist movements like Theosophy and the proto-nationalist Arya Samaj. The first Burmese chapter of the Arya Samaj was founded in Mandalay in 1897. "The urban Burmese interacted with this wide variety of interpretations and absorbed something of their approaches," writes Turner. This engagement proved short-lived. By the early 1900s, international movements had lost their appeal. Faced with a colonial regime that was not only extractive but violent—hungry for teak, gemstones, and Burmese bodies to fight its wars—Burmese Buddhists began to look inward. What had once been charitable Buddhist associations turned their efforts to resisting British rule. Religious identity began to blur into nationalism.

Among the most outspoken voices of the era was U Ottama, an Arakanese monk and follower of Gandhi, who toured the country delivering fiery speeches. The British, he declared, were "heathens" who had "robbed" and ruled "our land." If Burma's 80,000 monks made a "great push" for national freedom, he said, "we are sure to get it." U Ottama served as president of the Hindu Mahasabha, a precursor to the Rashtriya Swayamsevak Sangh, whose early leaders were inspired by Mussolini. He was—and remains—the only Buddhist to have led the Hindu nationalist group.

Another iconic figure was Saya San, a former monk who led a dagger-wielding rebellion that lasted a year and ended with his execution in 1931. A diminutive figure with hooded eyes, Saya San carried himself with a back as straight as an iron rod, and proclaimed himself king of Burma from a bamboo palace on a secluded hilltop. In an echo of events in Ceylon, Saya San's rebels targeted Indian homes and businesses.

After the British annexation of Burma, Indians could travel there freely and as often as they pleased. "Indians were far freer to set up their own businesses in Burma than in India," notes Mira Kamdar, whose family immigrated to Rangoon in the 1920s and 1930s. "They quickly became the principal landowners; moneylenders; merchants; rice millers; and, eventually, cinema owners and purveyors of every conceivable good and service in the land. At the other end of the economic spectrum, tens of thousands of workers were brought in from the poorer classes of India to perform the hard, menial labor in the mills, in the timber yards, and on the docks."

The exodus from India to Burma was driven less by choice than by colonial extraction: The British had systematically looted India's riches to fund its own industries, infrastructure, and wars, leaving millions of Indians on the edge of famine. Forced to seek work in distant imperial outposts—from Fiji to East Africa—some Indians found prosperity, but all were treated with suspicion and resentment. Anger at the British was deflected onto

Indians, who were seen as the middlemen of empire: more visible, more accessible, and easier to attack.

Saya San's rebellion exposed the ethnic fault lines that would later tear the country apart—first with Indians, many of them Muslim, and later with the Muslim Rohingya, who were accused of being Indian by virtue of their skin color and religion. Yet, his uprising also marked the rise of a new kind of figure: the charismatic monk-politician, whose moral authority could rouse a nation—and justify violence.

It was in these years that many Burmese began to see a startling transformation in the monastic order. The monks to whom they offered rice, bowed their heads, and whispered prayers were no longer just meditative figures in saffron robes. Increasingly, they became men who shouted slurs at Indians, looted shops, and incited—even joined in—acts of violence. The robe remained, but, for some, the role had changed.

Burma won its independence in 1948, but the euphoria was short-lived. Almost immediately, the country descended into a quagmire of ethnic strife. This unraveling occurred despite the fact that Buddhists comprised the majority of the population—and held, from the start, a tight grip on the levers of political, military, and economic power. Muslims, who today account for just 4 percent of the population, were openly and systematically treated as a threat. The bias was so deeply embedded that not a single Burmese Muslim I interviewed for this book could recall a time when it wasn't there. "They don't have a problem with the white men who enslaved them," one monk told me during an interview, flashing a dry smile. "But they have a problem with the brown man who lives beside them."

These tensions came to a head in 1962, when Ne Win, the supreme commander of the armed forces, seized power in a coup. He had begun his career as a postal clerk but was soon drawn into the nationalist movement, attending underground meetings and later joining the Burma Independence Army, founded by General Aung San, often called Burma's George Washington for his role in ending British colonial rule. Born Shu Maung, he renamed himself Ne Win, meaning "radiant sun," and rose to become one of Aung San's trusted lieutenants. After taking power, Ne Win launched the "Burmese Way to Socialism," a campaign sweeping in both its ambition and ruin. It nationalized nearly all private enterprises, shut down foreign trade, and expelled long-settled communities—many of whom had arrived during British rule, built businesses, raised families, taken Burmese names, and adopted the language. Among the expelled were nearly 400,000 Indians.

Aung Naing Soe, a thirty-four-year-old photographer who lives in exile in Mae Sot, was among those whose family was deeply affected. His Muslim grandparents were forced to return to Gujarat, India, he told me, and while his parents, who grew up in Rangoon, managed to stay back, they never felt truly safe. Later, they gave their children, including Aung, Burmese names to help them blend in. "The government never officially said we needed Burmese names to be registered in schools," he told me. "But we were never comfortable going out with our real names." His real name is Yaacoob.

Ne Win's radical xenophobia plunged Burma into isolationism, economic stagnation, and deeper unrest. In 1982, he introduced a citizenship law that redefined what it meant to be Burmese, formally recognizing 135 "indigenous" ethnic groups but excluding the Muslim Rohingya, who were concentrated in the western

Rakhine State, a deeply impoverished area that shares a border with Bangladesh. The Rohingya had lived here for generations; some historians traced their origins in the region to the fifteenth century. Following the law, however, many Rohingya who held national ID cards—confirming their citizenship—were forced to surrender them. Coupled with earlier crackdowns, these measures contributed to an exodus of more than 200,000 Rohingya into neighboring Bangladesh during the late 1970s and early 1990s.

Ne Win's law, notes Francis Wade, was inspired by "Britain's obsession with racial classification." It was the British who introduced the concept of a census based on ethnicity. And as with India and Ceylon, the British censuses created boundaries where, before, none had existed. In all three countries, the classification system defined who was considered pure and who could be discarded. And it furthered anti-Muslim sentiments, which led to anti-Muslim violence. These episodes, though not continuous or linear, show that British colonial policies helped create the conditions for religious nationalism, and that religious nationalism, in turn, often led to violence. Ne Win's law reinforced the notion that Rohingya—and, by extension, all Burmese Muslims, including those from the majority Bamar ethnicity—did not belong. It laid the groundwork for the genocidal violence that followed more than three decades later.

The first major anti-government demonstrations erupted in 1988, led by students who called for a nationwide general strike to bring down Ne Win's dictatorship. The mass event is often referred to as the "8888 Uprising" after the date, month, and year in which it began: August 8, 1988. At first, the students looked like they might succeed, but the military responded without mercy, shooting dead hundreds, if not thousands, of people.

Ne Win resigned, as the students had wanted, but his place was taken by the military through a junta called the State Law and Order Restoration Council. Later, SLORC changed its name to the State Peace and Development Council, and then changed the country's name from Burma to Myanmar, claiming that the former was a legacy of the British occupation. Many, including the people I interviewed for this book, still refer to it as Burma.

Among those the junta detained was Aung San Suu Kyi, the daughter of General Aung San. Suu Kyi lived in England, and was visiting Rangoon to look after her ailing mother. But, inspired by the students' courage, she decided to join them. "I could not as my father's daughter remain indifferent to all that was going on," she said in her first major public speech at the country's most revered Buddhist site—the iconic Shwedagon pagoda, a four-hundred-foot beacon clad in solid gold plates, once described by Somerset Maugham as a "sudden hope in the dark night." Speaking before an estimated 500,000 people, her address thrust her into the heart of Burmese politics and drew the attention of the world.

Placed under house arrest by the junta in July 1989, Suu Kyi occupied herself by reading, playing the piano, and meditating in her family villa on Inya Lake in Rangoon. In the monsoons she patched leaks. Beyond her property lines, and especially outside Myanmar's borders, she became a symbol of nonviolent resistance, drawing comparisons to figures like Gandhi and the Dalai Lama. In 1991, she was awarded the Nobel Peace Prize.

Yet, as with so much in Myanmar's complex political landscape, Suu Kyi's trajectory would eventually reveal far more nuance and controversy than her international image suggested.

"In Fear of Our Race Disappearing"

The monk I sought in Mae Sot lived on the balcony of an abandoned house, his only companion an old black dog. As he peered through his glasses at a tub of raw shrimp, the dog sat at his feet, eyes tender, nose twitching with hope. A kettle whistled. Garlic crackled in hot oil. The air was thick; sweat slid down Abbot Zero's face as he assembled a tea leaf salad. I wondered if the house was locked or if he simply couldn't bring himself to break in. His makeshift kitchen and bed were arranged out here, on the balcony where we stood. Nearby, a young Burmese exile, who would join us for the meal, smoked a cigarette. His gaze was fixed on the enormous sky and the matted green mountains. Beyond them lay his country.

Abbot Zero sat cross-legged on the chair beside me. Aung Naing Soe, the photographer, translated between us. "Let me know if the mosquitoes get too much for you," the monk said in Burmese. I looked at the forty-five-year-old man—his face unlined, his eyes clear and bright, despite the fact that he had endured imprisonment, starvation, and torture. *The junta wants to kill you,* I thought. You've fled your country. You're squatting on a balcony. And yet, you're worried about me.

Zero, the son of a farmer, had once been a university student with modest ambitions. That changed in 1996, when the latest wave of anti-government protests shut down his school. The demonstrations, which had begun in Yangon after security forces beat and detained some students, spread to Mandalay where he lived. Zero wanted nothing to do with politics, only for the unrest to end. As the closure dragged on, he turned to meditation to cope. "I became addicted," he said with a warm laugh. "It's inappropriate, but I kept wondering: How much can I meditate? How much peace can I gain? I also realized that meditation is complicated for someone with duties—to work, to feed himself, to have a family."

The protests widened to include other members of civil society. Protesters were loaded into trucks. They returned with split lips, bruised genitals, and ribs cracked under boots. Although the numbers of protesters swelled, poverty and isolation had made the transmission of news difficult. Many villages relied on a single crackling radio in a tea shop or monastery to listen to the BBC or the Democratic Voice of Burma. In this information vacuum, a nationwide uprising was impossible. With the prospect of true change dimming, Zero turned to the only path he believed could offer protection—or redemption. He became a monk.

Zero was in his twenties when he was ordained at Masoyein Monastery, a prestigious center of monastic scholarship. The monastery was known for its gilded columns and intricate carvings, as well as for its rock star monks—men who had mastered the Pali canon and drew crowds wherever they preached. Among them, one stood out. Ashin Wirathu was a magnet for attention, and Zero felt himself pulled into the older monk's orbit.

Eyes cast down, voice soft, responses always measured—Wirathu was then regarded as an intellectual. A senior monk, also on the run, who I later met in Mae Sot, described him to me as "brilliant" and "a natural." Wirathu wrote verses in praise of silence and discipline, helped compile a Pali dictionary, and built a library stocked with scripture, political treatises, and novels. He opened the monastery's doors to the outside world, inviting writers to give talks and students to study. "He wasn't the man he is today," Zero murmured. He was quiet for a moment. Then, almost to himself, he added: "I really respected him."

Little is known about Wirathu's early life beyond what he has chosen to share. Born in 1968 in Kyaukse, a town in Mandalay, he was one of eight children. His father, a tractor driver and water seller, traveled in an oxcart to earn a living, often bringing his son along. Wirathu was seventeen when he finally graduated the eighth grade, at which point his father sent him to a monastery for what was meant to be a brief stint, a rite of passage for Burmese Buddhist men. For Wirathu, it became a calling. "The Buddha's teachings," he told the Swiss director Barbet Schroeder in the 2017 documentary *The Venerable W.*, "were a peaceful domain without worry." He passed his exams and adapted to monastic discipline—one meal a day, cold-water baths, hours spent sitting on the wooden floor in study and recitation. His family was furious. "My father banged his head against the wall," Wirathu told Schroeder in a soporific tone. As the eldest son, his absence meant a loss of income.

In 1991, Wirathu moved to Masoyein Monastery, fifty kilometers away. The monastery housed over 2,000 novices, and twenty-three-year-old Wirathu went largely unnoticed. "When I fell ill, I was alone," he said. "I had to take care of myself." Each day, he carried his alms bowl through the streets, begging for food that was often barely edible. In the rigid hierarchy of the monastery, power was the only way to earn respect.

At the time, a monk at Yangon's Tant Kyi Taung Pagoda was drawing crowds with an unusual meditation technique. Grainy online videos show followers roaring like tigers and slithering like snakes. Intrigued but skeptical, Wirathu studied the Buddhist canon and concluded that the monk was a fraud. His response was a book, *The Path of the Theravada,* which he claimed the military banned, forcing him to self-publish. The book marked the beginning of his writing career and helped him attract followers outside the monastery. This elevated his position, and he was granted special privileges, invited to eat food with the more senior monks, and encouraged to take on a leadership role. Junior monks, including Zero, scurried alongside, eager to do his bidding.

In 1997, Wirathu's focus shifted to Islam. That year, he came across a clandestine pamphlet by an unknown author, *In Fear of Our Race Disappearing,* which warned that Muslims would overrun Myanmar unless stopped. Alarmed, he and a group of monks made it their mission to spread its message. They gave themselves code names—Wirathu was "The Patriot"—and met in secret, often at a nearby cemetery, disguising themselves in sunglasses and hoods made from their robes. Their speeches, which were recorded and circulated, called for action. Wirathu's sharp wit made him the movement's star. "The applause could reach the sky," he liked to boast. He warned that Muslims would soon outnumber the Bamar, Myanmar's largest ethnic group.

Rumors spread that Than Shwe, the junta leader, had taken notice.

Raised to believe that Myanmar belonged solely to Bamar Buddhists, Zero nodded along to Wirathu's rants. He remembered how, as a child, his parents had warned him that a Muslim man would snatch him away if he didn't finish his vegetables.

The slur *kalar*—akin to the N-word—was used to belittle Muslims and anyone with a darker complexion. It was a word that Burmese nationalists had hurled at Indians during British rule. The chant "Kala-Kala-Yaik-Yaik," or "Assault the foreigners," had been popularized by Buddhist monks who took part in the anti-Indian riots—looting, burning, and killing—in the years leading up to independence.

Zero heard the word thrown around casually. To his dismay, it was sometimes aimed at him because of his own skin tone. When Wirathu began reserving *kalar* exclusively for Muslims, Zero felt an unexpected sense of relief. Eager to show his admiration, he approached Wirathu whenever he could. The older monk took notice, and invited him to private meetings. Before long, Zero was part of Wirathu's inner circle.

Wirathu gave men like Zero a sense of belonging, identity, and confidence. Whoever they were—whatever the quality of their lives—at least they were not *kalar*. By positioning Muslims as an existential threat, he trained his followers to hate. He was no longer just a monk—he was their benevolent father, looking out for their best interests. Even when he spoke of things far removed from their daily struggles—the Bamiyan Buddhas, 9/11—his followers listened raptly; they trusted him completely.

When he asked, "Between a Buddhist and a Muslim, who should one prefer?"

Fellow monks, men and women, even children responded with full-throated enthusiasm: "The Buddhist!"

From his ornately decorated, elevated platform, Wirathu looked down upon the crowd. And what he saw below—hundreds, sometimes thousands, of faces turned upward—made him feel, Zero believed, like a god.

Offstage, Wirathu was an insatiable consumer of digital vitriol, spending hours online disseminating hate speech to his tens of thousands of Facebook followers. His cadre of assistants produced posters depicting unspeakable atrocities—dead children, mutilated bodies—labeled with proclamations such as "Victims of ISIS beheaded and arranged as a display for the media and public." Every available inch of wall space in Masoyein was claimed by his own photograph, transforming the premises into a shrine to his persona.

One day, he was just another monk. The next, he was on a national speaking tour—driven in a chauffeured SUV, flanked by a private security detail and trailed by a film crew. The origins of these lavish accoutrements—their funding, and the quid pro quo that secured them—were matters of speculation, but they were only ever whispered, never voiced aloud.

In September 2003, Wirathu delivered his most infamous speech yet, comparing Myanmar's Muslims to a fire that would consume the country unless extinguished. "I can't stand what they do to us," he said from behind a podium sprouting microphones. "What about you, venerables?"

"No!" the monks shouted back.

"So, listen to me carefully," he continued. "In a few days, I will make a decision. As soon as I give the signal, get ready to follow me."

His audience of scarlet-robed monks flashed broad smiles as they clapped and hooted their approval. Wirathu glowed under their adulation.

"I need to plan the operation well," he went on. "Like the CIA or Mossad, for it to be effective. . . . I will make sure the *kalars* have nothing to eat." The crowd hooted again. "And I will make sure they have nowhere to live."

More applause.

Zero was sitting in the crowd applauding as loudly as anyone else. And yet, as he told me over our lunch in Mae Sot, it was the first time he experienced a flicker of doubt. "Could I believe him?" he asked himself. "Were Muslims really that dangerous?"

On October 19 in Kyaukse, Wirathu's hometown, a stone struck a monastery compound during the end-of-Buddhist-Lent celebrations. Although no one was injured, the monks swiftly pointed to the neighboring mosque as the culprit. A mob swept through the town. In the ensuing violence, at least a dozen people died, including a pregnant woman. The riots soon spilled over into Mandalay, where Wirathu resided, and eventually reached the capital, Yangon. One report noted that the mobs reduced two mosques to rubble. Although the government later offered some compensation and authorized the rebuilding of the mosques, the reconstruction never materialized. By then, many of the Muslims of Kyaukse had fled.

In the broader history of anti-Muslim violence in the country, the events in Kyaukse are often relegated to a footnote, eclipsed by the more widespread brutality and, subsequently, the genocide that followed. Yet, it was in Kyaukse that Wirathu first demonstrated his capacity to mobilize monks to commit violence. In many respects, the town became his proving ground.

At the time, Wirathu was still a relatively obscure figure. His name was not yet known outside Myanmar. It would be another ten years before he appeared on the cover of *Time* magazine, and not until 2014 that he traveled to Sri Lanka, exchanging warm embraces with the leaders of the extremist Bodu Bala Sena. For now, the world remained unaware of Wirathu. That, too, was about to change.

Perhaps apprehensive that such potent mobilization might one day be turned against them, the junta reacted to the violence in Kyaukse by conducting searches of monasteries and arresting dozens of monks, including Wirathu. He was sentenced to twenty-five years for inciting anti-Muslim hatred, and incarcerated in the notorious Obo prison in Mandalay.

In nearby Masoyein, Wirathu's acolytes, Zero among them, protested on the streets, but security forces soon intervened to disperse them. Several monks were killed and many others were injured during the clashes. Zero narrowly escaped capture by scaling a high wall to return to the safety of his monastery. The series of events served as a stark reminder, Zero told me: Although Wirathu might have aligned himself with the military's views, neither he nor any monk in Myanmar was guaranteed protection from it.

Saffron Revolution

At 10:30 a.m. one morning in Mae Sot, Aung and I slipped off our shoes before entering the home of Maulvi Soe Nay Oo, an imam who had recently fled Myanmar. The family's morning ritual unfolded in the front room where a sparse breakfast of sliced white bread and tea was shared among neatly arranged chairs, a well-worn sewing machine, and a pile of crisply folded shirts. Modern conveniences were absent. The electricity, if it worked at all, was dormant despite the shimmering heat.

A compact man of forty years with a weatherbeaten face, Soe Nay walked up to a map on the wall. "This is where I was born," he said, pointing to Sagaing, in the southwest of Mandalay, an area now controlled by resistance forces—a matter of pride for the imam. "This is Mandalay," he continued, showing me the district that carried Wirathu's imprimatur. "And this," he said with something of a sigh, slowly dragging his finger across the map's eastern edge toward the Burmese border with Thailand, "is where I have come to hide."

He sat on the floor with his hands on his knees. He had grown up working alongside his parents who sold Buddhist amulets from a cart, he told me. His earliest memories include being labeled a *kalar* and taunted by friends. "*Kalar, kalar,* eat my shit," they would say, surrounding him and aiming kicks at his shins. There was a hierarchy, and people who looked like him, and prayed at mosques, were at the bottom—of this he was aware. He believed monks stood at the top. They could be kind—Soe Nay had seen it himself whenever a monk stopped by the cart to ruffle his hair and chat with his parents. They were powerful. While selling amulets outside monasteries, he watched flashy cars carrying military leaders pull up to the gates, bringing lacquered trays loaded with lotus flowers and glistening fruit. And they could be cruel. He remembers arriving at a monastery with a basket of his own modest offering—just a few apples—only to be told by the very monk whose blessing he sought to sit at a distance because he was "unworthy."

Recalling the moment, Soe Nay rocked back and forth, gripping his knees.

In the summer of 2007, when Soe Nay was twenty-three, news arrived of a ruckus in the capital, Yangon, where a group of earnest-looking men, holding placards in a bustling fruit and vegetable market, shouted, "People are suffering! The government is doing nothing! Take to the streets and join us." Their protest—like so many in Myanmar—was brief. Security officers in crisp white shirts and black trousers swiftly apprehended and bundled them away.

They had been protesting a fivefold rise in fuel prices introduced that month, at the height of the rainy season. The sharp hike made it nearly impossible for many to afford the bus to work—and then, because they couldn't work, to buy even staples like rice and eggs. Families began bringing their children to monasteries for meals.

Meanwhile, photographs surfaced of the wedding of junta leader Than Shwe's daughter draped in diamonds and pearls, perched on a gold-trimmed chair. The reception was awash in champagne and guests feasted on a five-tiered cake.

When the protesters remained in prison, a group of monks in a town near Mandalay took to the streets. "It's the monks," passersby murmured in astonishment. "The monks are joining." Although they marched in silence, the police still beat them. Senior monks demanded an apology, which never came. By mid-September, thousands of monks had gone on strike in a profound act of defiance that virtually emptied out the country's monasteries. To many, the monks' participation underscored the gravity of the moment. Myanmar is home to 400,000 monks, and it seemed as if every one of them was now on the streets.

In Mandalay, where he lived, Soe Nay watched with a mix of hope and apprehension. The country was bent double under the weight of the junta's demands and everyday life was even more precarious for Muslims. Perhaps this protest, Soe Nay thought, would be different. Monks, he told himself, understood politics.

At Masoyein Monastery nearby, the monk Zero was thinking along similar lines. He had kept a low profile since Wirathu's arrest four years earlier. But now, he thought, was the time to awaken, to act. He, too, left his monastery.

From Yangon to Mandalay, and soon in cities and towns across the country, robed monks walked in solemn procession, chanting the Metta Sutta, a discourse on loving-kindness and compassion. Its verses echoed their message: "Let no one ever deceive another. Nor disparagingly look upon another anywhere. Either in anger or in hostility, let no people wish the unhappiness of one another."

And then:

"Whatever living [breathing] things there are, all of those that tremble and those that are steady and strong . . . those that live near or afar . . . may all those living things be blissful and happy."

The internet, satellite dishes, mobile phones, and video cameras—technologies once out of reach—were now widely available in Myanmar. For the first time, Burmese people could capture breaking news as it happened and share it. Dubbed the Saffron Revolution—after the color of some of the monks' robes—the protest captured the world's imagination with its promise of good triumphing over evil. These very modern revolutionaries made the cover of *The Economist*, in a story that declared: "If the world acts in concert, the violence [of the military] should be the last spasm of a vicious regime in its death throes." In another sign that change was underway, Aung San Suu Kyi was permitted to open the gate of her courtyard and greet the monks. As the rain poured down, she responded to their prayers with tears in her eyes.

Then the monks took yet another radical step: They refused to perform rituals, or accept food, from government officials, army officers, and even the families of military personnel. Historian Thant Myint-U called it "an exceptionally serious step in a fervently religious society."

Inevitably, the junta struck back. Although soldiers had previously beaten monks, they had never attacked them with such viciousness. Now they shot to kill or they hauled monks to prison and defrocked them. No one knows how many died. Dozens, some say; a hundred, according to others.

The Saffron Revolution was a profound event in the history of Myanmar—and in the story of politically engaged Buddhism—restoring to monks a measure of moral and political power. By then, the Tibetan resistance had lost momentum. After decades of Chinese rule, Beijing's control was deeply entrenched. Monasteries were shuttered or destroyed and religious practice was under relentless surveillance. One of the most consequential moves was China's unilateral appointment of its own Panchen Lama—the second-highest figure in Tibetan Buddhism—a position chosen by the Dalai Lama. The child recognized by the Dalai Lama as the rightful Panchen Lama was taken into custody in 1995 and has not been seen since. Today, even images of the Dalai Lama are banned in Tibet.

The Saffron Revolution cut through the despair. It reminded Buddhists—and the world—that monks could still galvanize change, that their moral authority could indeed stir the masses. Watching from the Dharamshala mountains, the Tibetan government in exile recognized this shift. The Dalai Lama issued a statement of solidarity: "I fully support their call for freedom and democracy and take this opportunity to appeal to freedom-loving people all over the world to support such non-violent movements."

For monks like Zero—marching for the first time for their country—and for citizens like Soe Nay Oo—who had experienced persecution—the peaceful demonstrations kindled a brief, vivid hope.

Wirathu was released in January 2012, as part of a general amnesty for political prisoners, after serving only nine years of his sentence. Back at Masoyein, he transformed his monastic quarters into a war room. Tables were strewn with laptops, where monks scrolled through the news, updated Wirathu's multiple social media feeds, and organized public meetings. It was from here that he masterminded his latest scheme: an economic boycott targeting Muslim businesses.

The movement was christened "969," a numerical shorthand for the three jewels of Buddhism: the nine qualities of the Buddha, the six key teachings of the Dharma, and the nine virtues of the Sangha, the monastic community. It was also a riposte to "786," a number used by Muslims in Myanmar to signify the Arabic phrase, "In the name of God, the most gracious, the most merciful." Groups of 969 supporters distributed stickers that featured Buddhist imagery such as the four lions associated with Emperor Ashoka, who revived and spread Buddhism across South and Southeast Asia. These stickers were then plastered on businesses to identify them as Buddhist-owned, and supporters were urged to shop only at 969-endorsed establishments.

Several people I spoke to suggested that Wirathu's movement was no grassroots uprising but part of a military strategy to destabilize Myanmar. "The military wants to create constant chaos," Zero said. "To distract people." By manufacturing an enemy, the military could justify its role as protector. It needed foes to rally against and to defeat.

Wirathu's rise had unfolded against a backdrop of transformation, or so it seemed. In 2011, the military ceded power to a quasi-civilian government led by former junta leader turned President Thein Sein. Sanctions were lifted, and Myanmar's economy opened to the world. Mobile penetration, once just

5 percent, soared. Global giants like Google, GE, and Microsoft circled. Malls rose in Yangon. Netflix and Burger King followed.

For the United States, Myanmar represented more than just a burgeoning market—strategically located between India and China, it was also a geopolitical prize. With China's influence growing, Washington was keen to forge alliances. In December 2011, Secretary of State Hillary Clinton visited Myanmar, engaging in talks with Thein Sein and dining privately with Aung San Suu Kyi. Previously released from house arrest, Suu Kyi had initially resisted entering politics, citing the junta's lingering grip on power. After her meeting with Clinton, she declared her intention to assume a more active political role. "I think our way ahead will be clearer," she said, in her distinctive British-accented English, as Clinton, standing beside her, beamed. "And we will be able to trust that the process of democratization will go forward."

Despite the reforms, daily life in Myanmar remained steeped in uncertainty. Thein Sein's government, though nominally civilian, was dominated by ex-soldiers who courted prominent monks in an effort to formalize an alliance between the country's two most powerful institutions. Sitagu Sayadaw—a deeply revered monk who had supported the 1988 pro-democracy uprising—now referred to the country's Muslims as "guests" and Buddhists as "hosts." "The guests must obey the hosts," he warned. By day, robed monks could be seen on the streets shouting, "Rohingya, go home!" By night, the same figures were spotted in karaoke bars, smoking and absorbed in their smartphones.

Over lunch, I asked Zero, "Why did so many monks switch sides?"

He gave a small, apologetic smile. "They're just village boys, like me. They don't read. They don't think beyond the end of the day. They follow whoever leads. And Wirathu is a brilliant man who knows how to make people feel what he says."

Isolation shaped them, too. For decades, Myanmar had turned inward, its monks marooned from the wider Buddhist world. Only Sri Lanka remained within reach where groups like Bodu Bala Sena offered not only connection but confirmation, shoring up a shared belief in purity and peril. A report by the Crisis Group traced the echo: "Religious exchanges with Sri Lanka . . . reinforced nationalist narratives and fears of a global Islamist terrorist threat."

In his first major speech after getting out of prison, Wirathu described the Masoyein monastery as a "rampart" for Theravada, the orthodox form of Buddhism practiced in the country. "The monks must be an army who fight on the front line," he declared.

The turning point came on a hot, dry day in May 2012, when a Buddhist seamstress in Rakhine State was found raped and killed, allegedly by Rohingya men. The police arrested three suspects, but retaliation was broad and swift. A mob of three hundred Rakhine Buddhists dragged ten Muslim men off a bus and beat them to death. Days later, Muslim residents set fire to Buddhist properties. The violence spiraled. In footage I reviewed, flames consumed villages, smoke darkened the skies, and caravans of Rohingya families fled Rakhine with whatever they could carry. Within hours, over 100,000 people were displaced.

As Rakhine descended into anarchy, Wirathu's monks distributed a propaganda DVD featuring images of the seamstress's body.

I learned what happened next from MT, a Burmese politician I met for dinner at her home in Mae Sot. She asked to use only her initials fearing reprisals from the junta. By "home," I mean two cramped rooms—no running water, no modern toilet—alongside half a dozen cats. She had adopted them since fleeing Myanmar in 2023 with the help of human traffickers, who took all her wedding jewelry in exchange. She had since bought a secondhand sewing machine and makes her living mending clothes.

As we shared a meal, MT cradled two of her cats in her lap—one wore a T-shirt, the other had a bell around its neck—and fed them shreds of beef. As though reading my mind, she confided that this was her third house in Mae Sot. Speaking to Aung, the photographer, in Burmese, she said, "The others were even worse."

In 2013, MT was serving as the head of the National League for Democracy's Meiktila chapter. It was dangerous work. The previous year, the NLD had claimed a historic victory in the by-elections, securing Aung San Suu Kyi her first seat in Parliament after nearly two decades under house arrest. Though the regime outwardly accepted the results, its displeasure was palpable, and those aligned with the NLD knew that reprisal was only a matter of time. More troubling still were Suu Kyi's statements to the international press, which revealed her unwillingness to challenge the military. Only weeks after the 2012 violence in Rakhine State, she described the bloodshed as merely a failure of "the rule of law." When asked whether the Rohingya should be granted citizenship, she had hesitated. "I don't know," she said.

Increasingly, MT felt there was no one to turn to. There were no saviors in Myanmar, only bullies, their collaborators, and finally, people like her.

Sure enough, in February 2013, Wirathu arrived in Meiktila with his band of 969 supporters. A large trading town south of Mandalay, Meiktila had a population of about 170,000, roughly

30 percent of whom were Muslim. Many Muslims ran thriving businesses, particularly in car repair—a success that may have fueled Wirathu's resentment. According to MT, his speech was entirely "anti-Muslim." Her account reminded me of Fazeena Fihar, the Muslim teacher in Sri Lanka who had narrowly escaped an anti-Muslim riot led by monks—a near-identical script, vilifying Muslims as a threat only to grab property.

After Wirathu departed, pamphlets appeared in the markets claiming that Burmese Buddhists in Meiktila were "living in terror" of the "*kalars*." "We are terrified when we see a large group of *kalars* going to the mosque every day. We would like to appeal to the monks for help." It was signed "Buddhists of Meiktila," and an addendum insisted, "This letter is not intended to create riots or political instability. It is distributed so that the love of the nation and the religion may live for a long time."

MT and her eight siblings, whose homes stood close together, devised a plan: If violence broke out, they would run to one home and hide. They stored their vehicles elsewhere and stashed valuables and paperwork. Within days, on March 20, 2013, a quarrel between a Buddhist family and a Muslim shopkeeper segued into a riot during which police stood idle, monks acted as provocateurs, and rioters wielding swords pranced in jubilation. "Oooh! Look how many of them. Kill them! Kill them!" they shouted.

The bloodlust claimed at least twenty children, one of whom was decapitated, while another was set on fire. In footage captured by the BBC, a monk repeatedly strikes a child lying helpless in a field. Another monk held a blade to the throat of an Associated Press photographer, demanding his camera's memory card. Witnesses saw monks force Muslims to kneel on the ground and worship them.

Not all monks joined the mayhem. Sayadaw U Visudda of Meiktila's Yadanar Oo Monastery made headlines for protecting hundreds of Muslims. "If you really want them, you'll have to get through me," he told a mob trying to break in. "I accepted [the Muslims] according to the Metta principle [of loving-kindness] of the Lord Buddha," he later explained to *Frontier Myanmar*. "You should save anyone who is in trouble. They [Muslims] have been living here for centuries. In normal times, there was no reason for conflict; what happened was deliberate." In Lashio, at the Thiri Mingalar Mansu Shan Monastery, senior monk Sayadaw U Pannananda also sheltered hundreds, offering them food and bedding, and speaking to the police on their behalf.

MT finally reached her sister's house, where she spent a terrified night listening to explosions and screams. By morning, she and her siblings feared they would be burned alive. When they tried to slip out, they were confronted by monks on motorbikes. "They tried to chop people," she said. "We just ran until we reached the sports stadium, where hundreds of others were trying not to die." When the riots subsided and MT's family returned, they found all nine of their homes reduced to ash. They spent the rest of the year in a displacement camp.

While Meiktila burned, the attention of the Western media was fixed on Eric Schmidt, then Google's executive chairman, who was in Yangon on what he called a fact-finding mission. Tanned and cheerful, Schmidt spoke at a technical university, where he urged students not to let the government control the internet, as though that choice belonged to them. "Try to keep the government out of regulating the internet," he said. "The answer to bad speech is more speech. More communication." The disconnect between upbeat Western narratives of Myanmar's reforms and the reality on the ground could not have been more apparent.

The violence in Meiktila rolled on from township to township, each flare-up following the same deadly pattern: "Rumors of a Muslim harming a Buddhist woman or a monk igniting mass anger and bloodshed," as historian Thant Myint-U put it. By June 2013, riots led by Buddhist mobs across the country had killed more than two hundred Muslims and forced at least 150,000 people—most of them Muslim—from their homes.

A few days after Meiktila's conflagration, the BBC's Jonathan Head interviewed Wirathu at his temple in Mandalay. "When you leave a seed from a tree to grow in the pagoda," the monk said, "it seems so small at first. But you know you must cut it out before it grows and destroys the building."

When I asked MT about Wirathu's statement, she tipped her head back and let out a sigh. The cats in her lap mewed. Her siblings were still in Myanmar, she told me. She'd cut off contact—even unfriending them on Facebook—to avoid fueling the military's suspicions about her escape. Though she was in another country, fear clung to her.

"I can't sleep at night," she said. "I'm afraid they'll come for me."

As I stood to leave, MT continued scrolling through pictures on her phone. Every so often, she would hold the screen in front of my face, as though to say: *This is who I really am.*

In one photograph, she pauses with fellow NLD workers after the successful 2012 elections. She's wearing lipstick, a necklace, a vibrantly patterned sarong. Her face is radiant.

"Global Muslim Power Is Very Great"

As Meiktila struggled to recover, Wirathu found yet another cause to champion. He became obsessed with drafting a set of laws around race and religion, which he urged the government of Thein Sein to adopt. The laws would restrict interfaith marriage and religious conversion, ban polygamy, and impose family-planning measures in areas where the state deemed the population "abnormally high." Given Wirathu's views on the Rohingya, it was hardly a stretch to see the provisions as a direct assault on the community's right to have families. "Over a million Bengalis have crossed our borders illegally. They want to take over Rakhine," Wirathu said, once again making claims that were at odds with verifiable records.

After a UN human rights official warned that the laws could signal a regression in Myanmar's political reforms, Wirathu rallied an audience to jeer at her. "Just because you hold a position at the United Nations doesn't make you an honorable woman. In our country, you are just a whore," Wirathu said, to cheers and laughter from the crowd. "If you are so willing, you should offer your arse to the *kalar*. But you will never sell off our Arakan State!"

By 2014, Wirathu's 969 movement had evolved into the Ma Ba Tha—the Association for the Protection of Race and Religion. It became a professionally run organization with a central committee, regional offices, and a network of volunteers focused on disseminating propaganda. Ma Ba Tha launched an expansive communications strategy that included newspapers, cable television programs, and a steady output of posters and pamphlets portraying Muslims as perpetrators of global violence. These materials were distributed at markets, bus stops, and monasteries. One popular video featured a 969 monk leading a crowd in a raucous singalong of the group's anthem, "We Will Fence the Country with Our Bone." The lyrics called Muslims "ungrateful creatures" who "drink our water . . . break our rules . . . [and] destroy our youth."

Ma Ba Tha grew so influential that it successfully pushed Wirathu's race and religion laws through Parliament in 2015, backed by Thein Sein's Union Solidarity and Development Party. Its success, analysts noted, stemmed in part from its ability to step in where the state had failed. It opened Buddhist Sunday schools, provided legal aid, and offered disaster relief, positioning itself as a community aid organization. To many, it became indispensable. Notably, its appeal extended to Buddhist nuns as well as laywomen, some of whom cited feminist ideals as their reason for joining. A Crisis Group report observed that many Buddhist women were drawn to the group because of its commitment to ending polygamy. This blend of social outreach and nationalist ideology magnified Ma Ba Tha's influence, and also aligned its activities with those of groups abroad, such as India's

Hindu nationalist Rashtriya Swayamsevak Sangh and Arya Samaj.

In 2015, Wirathu returned the favor by making more than two dozen public appearances across Myanmar, including in the volatile Rakhine State, where he urged crowds to support Thein Sein's party in the upcoming elections. According to the Burmese Muslim Association, these visits included meetings with anti-Muslim group leaders and appeals for cash donations. In an already uneven election, Ma Ba Tha members threatened opposition politicians and pressured police and judges to fall in line. The conflict and research group C4ADS described the Ma Ba Tha as enjoying "unrivaled freedom" during the elections to do as they pleased.

At the same time, Wirathu courted international media attention, embracing provocative nicknames coined by foreign journalists—"the Burmese Bin Laden" and "the bald Neo-Nazi." In an interview with *The Times* of London, he expressed admiration for the far-right English Defence League. "We would like to be like the EDL," he said. "Not carrying out violence but protecting the public."

But decades of protests, access to social media, creeping globalization, and Suu Kyi's unstoppable rise gave the Nobel Prize winner's National League for Democracy (NLD) a momentum that even Ma Ba Tha couldn't stop.

In November 2015, the NLD won a landslide victory in the general elections to form Myanmar's first non-military government in fifty-four years. Suu Kyi was forbidden from holding the title of president, on the manufactured excuse that her children and spouse were foreign nationals. Instead, she assumed the newly created role of state counselor. Yet, real power remained out of reach: The military, and key ministries, remained under the command of Senior General Min Aung Hlaing—a dour, ruthless figure known among his academy peers as "cat poop." He and Suu Kyi rarely spoke.

The NLD's victory was further marred by its exclusion of Muslim candidates. Most of the country's Muslims—particularly the Rohingya—had already been disenfranchised and barred from participating in the elections. In an interview with the BBC shortly before the vote, Suu Kyi was once again given the chance to condemn the violence that had become woven into the fabric of her nation. Once again, she declined. "Muslims have been targeted, but Buddhists have also been subjected to violence," she told the BBC's Mishal Husain. Global Muslim power, she added, was "very great."

For Abbot Zero, it was this refusal—so public, so pointed—that jolted him from what he would later describe as a "stupor." The silence of Suu Kyi, the moral failure of the new government, and the escalating bigotry around him became impossible to ignore. "My fellow Bamar Buddhists," he told me, "were poisoning the atmosphere, and no one was willing to stop them." He began leaving the monastery more frequently, traveling across Mandalay to meet members of the Muslim community. He asked how they were feeling, what they had endured. He listened. He documented. He began to gather testimonies with the intent of crafting a counternarrative—one that could push back against the dangerous propaganda flooding the country through the internet, and now widely accepted as truth.

Two pivotal events would soon alter the course of Zero's life—events that would ultimately lead to his imprisonment and exile.

On October 9, 2016, insurgents in Rakhine State attacked three police posts, killing nine border officers. General Min Aung Hlaing's soldiers responded by setting dozens of Rohingya villages ablaze. As the military launched shoulder-fired rockets, families fled across the border into Bangladesh. A young Burmese lieutenant, deployed to Rakhine with hundreds of troops, described his experience on social media: "In our plane, we got to eat cake," he posted. "Are you going to eat Bengali meat?" asked one commenter. Another replied, "Crush the *kalar*, buddy." The lieutenant answered: "Will do." Later, he added: "If they're Bengali, they'll be killed." The following August, Rohingya insurgents struck again, attacking around thirty police posts and an army camp. According to Suu Kyi's government, eleven security personnel were killed. This time, the military went on a rampage. Survivors described women raped, children—including infants—beaten to death, and men systematically murdered, their bodies doused in gasoline and set on fire.

Leila Begum, a housewife, recounted her ordeal to CNN:

> The military entered our village and started shooting. It was chaos, everyone running in different directions. My sons got separated from me. My husband was nearby, but the military caught him and stabbed him—right beside me. I didn't see exactly what happened to my sons, but after the soldiers left, we found their bodies on the ground. My two daughters had stayed close to me, so they survived. We slept in the forest for four days, then walked two days through the mountains to Bangladesh. I cried the whole way. When we reached the border, we had to step over three dead bodies that had been shot not long before.

Another survivor, Nur Begum, described being rounded up and taken into the bushes. "A soldier cut off a woman's breast," she said. "He held it up like this and showed us, and it was shaking. He said if we screamed, they would do the same to us." Then, she said, several soldiers raped her.

Across the country, an estimated 9,000 Rohingya were killed. International observers condemned the violence as ethnic cleansing. Amnesty International called it a "scorched earth" campaign. United Nations investigators later concluded that Myanmar's military had acted with genocidal intent. More than 700,000 Rohingya—over 80 percent of Myanmar's Rohingya population—were forced into neighboring Bangladesh, reaching it only after a hazardous trek through jungles, over mountains, and across the Naf River, where many drowned. Those who survived arrived at Cox's Bazar, a dilapidated town already hosting tens of thousands of Rohingya refugees from earlier waves of violence. In the camps, female-headed households predominated. The women, traumatized and vulnerable, became prey for sex traffickers. Many would eventually risk another escape—boarding rickety boats in the hope of reaching Malaysia, Indonesia, or Thailand.

Throughout the genocide, Facebook played a pivotal role in spreading misinformation and disinformation. As of June 2017, Myanmar had approximately 15 million Facebook users—yet the platform had no staff based in the country and employed only one Burmese-speaking content moderator, located in Dublin. By contrast, Facebook had assigned hundreds of moderators to countries like China. On September 1, 2017, Senior General Min Aung Hlaing posted on his verified Facebook page: "We openly declare that absolutely, our country has no Rohingya race." The post remained online. So did countless others by Wirathu, who likened Muslims to dogs, claimed they "breed like rabbits," and portrayed them as terrorists and rapists. "If the internet had not come to [Myanmar], not many people would know my opinion and messages like now," Wirathu told BuzzFeed.

Amnesty International concluded that Meta had "substantially contributed" to the genocide by amplifying content designed to incite violence. The human rights group called on Facebook to provide reparations to the Rohingya—a demand to which Meta did not respond, although the company later acknowledged its failure to act.

In her insider account *Careless People*, published in 2025, Sarah Wynn-Williams, a former director of global public policy at Facebook, acknowledged that the company had refused to ban the slur *kalar*, declined to remove hate speech on the grounds that it did not violate local law, and allowed Wirathu's Ma Ba Tha to operate freely. "The truth here is inescapable," Wynn-Williams wrote. "Myanmar would've been far better off if Facebook had never arrived." It was on Facebook, too, that Suu Kyi's fall from grace was completed. At the height of the genocide, her office circulated posts indistinguishable from those shared by the extremists, including images that purported to show Rohingya burning their own homes. Many of these images had already been debunked, yet they remained online.

In December 2019, Suu Kyi appeared before the International Court of Justice in The Hague, where she dismissed allegations of genocide as "incomplete and misleading." For those who had once seen her as a symbol of defiance against military oppression, it was a final, irrevocable betrayal. In a camp across the border in Bangladesh, Abdul Rahim, a Rohingya refugee, shook his head. "She is a liar. A great liar," he told Reuters. "Shame on her."

The violence in Rakhine seemed almost otherworldly—but it was not. Zero wanted to travel there to help the Rohingya but was dissuaded by fellow monks, who warned that his presence might be misinterpreted. Instead, he began organizing peaceful protests from within the monastery. Not all his peers believed the Rohingya were entitled to equal rights, or that they were as Burmese as the Bamar, but they agreed on one thing: The violence was indefensible. "Now that you've adopted the cat—or the dog—you don't kick it," one monk told Zero. "What's done is done."

The junta had defrocked dissenting monks in the past, but Zero and his group decided to protest anyway, walking barefoot and bareheaded out of their temple each day with their alms bowls tucked under their arms—a now well-understood symbol of defiance. This was when Zero adopted his activist name. His chosen moniker reflected his Buddhist belief in letting go of ego, a willingness to erase his own identity to alleviate the suffering of others. He became Ashin, or Venerable, Zero, a monk dedicated to justice.

The year 2021 dawned, and with it came yet another change of fortune for the monk Zero, and for his country. He and his fellow dissidents had begun demonstrating nearly four years earlier, after the genocide began, and had taken to the streets every day, every month, and every year since. This daily protest was now a part of Zero's life. Then, early one morning, he and his fellow monks were ambushed on the streets of Mandalay.

Zero was taken aback at having finally drawn the military's attention. He hesitated, and as he tried to flee, he stumbled, falling on his knees with an agonizing crack, his alms bowl slipping out of his hands and rolling away. The soldiers hauled him into a dusty black pickup truck. The events of that day, later known as Bloody Saturday, were part of a nationwide crackdown that claimed the lives of more than a hundred people.

By now the junta had once again seized control, thrown Suu Kyi into prison, and pulled the country back into the shadows of dictatorship. At the helm now was Suu Kyi's nemesis, General Min Aung Hlaing, who had spearheaded the violence against the Rohingya. Security forces arrested, tortured, and disappeared people. "They are killing us like birds or chickens, even in our homes," said one protester. Monks were treated like anyone else; witnesses described them being run over by military vehicles. The images were widely circulated as a warning to other members of the clergy.

There was, however, at least one known exception: Ashin Wirathu.

Imprisoned in 2020 on charges of sedition against Suu Kyi's government, he was released by the junta the very next year. General Min Aung Hlaing was reported to have lavished the disgraced cleric with honors and cash, and even awarded him a national accolade. The general publicly feted Wirathu for his "outstanding work for the good of the Union of Myanmar." Now in his late fifties, Wirathu was, at the time of writing, keeping a low profile—banned from Facebook and largely out of sight. Still, stories about him abounded, and they had taken a darker turn. A monk I met in Mae Sot claimed the junta had him hooked on drugs; the last time he heard Wirathu preach, he said, the notorious extremist's eyes were glassy. Whether such accounts were fact, idle gossip, or wishful thinking was impossible to tell. What was clear, though, was that the man who had once galvanized a movement was now a shadow of his former self.

Meanwhile, Zero was convicted by a kangaroo court in an abandoned schoolyard and sentenced to three years in prison. Stripped of his monastic robes, he was thrown into a communal ward, he told me, alongside convicted murderers and rapists. "It was so crowded we had to take turns lying down to sleep," he said. "And we were chained at all times—like animals." Like the others, Zero urinated into a bucket, defecated into plastic bags, and when he fell ill, his pleas for medical help were ignored. As spring turned to summer, the cell—devoid of even a fan—grew stifling. Then the water ran out. Zero pooled his money with other prisoners to bribe the guards for tanker deliveries. With what remained, he bought himself a spot in the corner, away from the suffocating crush. "It was hell," he said.

He was released two years later for what a court called "good behavior." A photograph from that day shows a frail man in a faded purple longyi and worn slippers, clutching a few bottles of water as a small group of friends gathers around him outside the prison gates. The image—hopeful, yet haunting—quickly made the rounds on social media. "A prominent Buddhist monk (U Zin Zero) has been released!" one supporter wrote. "Despite the junta ripping off his robes during his unjust imprisonment, he still carries the spirit of a monk in the way he wears the longyi. But let us not forget: many others are still being persecuted, arrested, and even killed in #Myanmar." In fact, a monk released on the same day as Zero had already been picked up by the junta and thrown immediately back in prison.

Zero had no intention of courting imprisonment again. His escape, meticulously planned over three weeks and executed in silence, was a secret shared only with a close friend and his ailing mother—they alone knew that he had paid a human trafficker to whisk him across the border into Thailand. He took a last selfie with the friend and said a final goodbye to his mother. It was in Thailand, in the summer of 2024, that I met him deep in the jungle, his once-loyal entourage reduced to a solitary stray dog.

After the junta seized power in 2021, hundreds of guerrilla groups took up arms. The country descended into chaos, with even the army's opponents—particularly in Rakhine State—facing accusations from international aid organizations of abuses against civilians, including killings, sexual violence, and forced recruitment.

Zero could see his homeland across the mountains, but the prospect of returning seemed remote. I asked if he had any regrets, though I already suspected the answer. Zero grinned. "Yes," he said, with a hint of mischief. "I wish I had protested more." It was the truth, he implied, and also how he preferred our conversation to end—by suggesting that things were not as dire as they seemed. He confided that he expected his mother to pass away soon, and he knew he would not be with her. Being a monk, he suggested, did not simplify his choices or absolve him of guilt. "I have never caused her trouble," he said. "But I have also never been much help."

Even from Thailand, though, Zero stayed in the fight. He created anonymous accounts to counter military propaganda, calling out false reports and circulating evidence of abuses. In Mae Sot, he led prayers for the dead and missing with other monks in exile, keeping the memory of resistance alive. He helped organize fundraisers for displaced families, moving money across borders where he could. Exile had not ended his role—it had forced him to adapt.

After our meeting with Zero, Aung and I found ourselves with some time before our next interview. He suggested visiting a monastery in Mae Sot—an elegant structure perched on a hill. At the summit, one monk lit a cigarette while another, seated nearby and petting a dog, offered a brief smile. A rustling prompted me to glance down, half-expecting to see snakes. To my left, the town spread out; to my right flowed the Moei River. Across the water in Myanmar, the garish white lights of scam compounds held trafficked men and women forced to defraud strangers; factories churned out whiskey and Absolut; casinos served Chinese tourists; and beyond all this lay the Dawna mountains in Karen State, where hundreds of militia soldiers were locked in battle with the junta.

Below, on the Thai side, the inky black forests offered refuge to those who had crossed the border with nowhere to call home. Aung explained that the jungle harbored a motley mix of families on the run, lone child soldiers, traffickers, corrupt police, and humanitarian workers scrambling to deliver medicine, blankets, and food. I couldn't see much, but I heard the howling of dogs. Standing there, I saw the entire tapestry of the story I had been chasing—from the epicenter of violence to pockets of escape, relief, and perhaps redemption.

As the sun set, the monks returned to the monastery with the dog at their side. Aung and I walked back to the car and drove into town, where few streetlights punctuated the darkness. In the distance, the sound of gunfire drifted across the water.

Part Three

Thailand

Nation, Religion, Monarchy

The monsoon had come to Bangkok. It rained all day and all night. The sound, like static, filled my ears. Soon, I found myself struggling to shake off the drowsiness that settles over the city this time of year. Each morning, I woke to a dense gray sky through which the neon billboards of the skyline pulsed faintly, their colors dulled by cloud and rain. On the Chao Phraya River, waves climbed higher, slapping the sides of the ferry and splashing passengers in the face.

One evening, I joined the crowds crossing to the western bank to visit Wat Arun, the Temple of the Dawn. It was impossible to miss—over two hundred feet high, crowned by a central tower and four golden spires that caught and scattered the sun. Its surface glittered with porcelain tiles said to have been salvaged from a shipwreck.

At the pier, I paid 200 baht (around $6) for a ticket and walked beneath a builder's scaffolding to reach the temple's entrance. Banyan trees with bleached white roots stood sentry. What I stepped into wasn't the solemn grandeur I expected, but something closer to Disneyland. The grounds were thick with people dressed as characters from Thai history—kings and queens, sturdy young princes, tiny princesses in gauzy pink dresses and golden shoes, trying their best not to slip on the rain-slicked ground. Some of the men wore plasticky armor, which they carried with a kind of nervous pride, as though preparing for a battle. The women floated by under parasols. All around were the familiar trappings of modern Asian tourism: machines selling T-shirts, a man hawking lottery tickets, vendors pressing key chains into the hands of passersby.

Bangkok is one of the world's great tourist cities, so it wasn't surprising that foreigners made up most of the crowd, or that they came equipped with all the usual gear—selfie sticks, battery-operated fans, Stanley water bottles. But as they moved up and down the steps, photographing themselves against the backdrop of devotion, I noticed the pilgrims struggling to complete their circumambulation. While the tourists arrived with cameras, the pilgrims came with candles. They bowed before the temple, lit incense sticks, placed them by flickering flames at an altar, and laid down lotus stems in prayer. The tourists, meanwhile, scrambled up the steep steps toward the spires and giggled as they pressed their cheeks to statues of angels, demons, and monkeys—representing heaven, hell, and earth. Later, I would learn that many of the tourists were Chinese content creators inspired to visit Thailand by the popularity of *Love Destiny*, a Thai TV drama set in the historic capital of Ayutthaya.

A monk's voice echoed from loudspeakers across the compound. I assumed it was a recording—until he paused mid-sermon to say, in English, "Hello, hello, welcome everyone, I am Buddhist monk. Happy, happy." But aside from his voice, there were few monks in sight. One, seated on a raised platform, accepted gift baskets overflowing with soap, shampoo, and lotion—items sold at the temple itself. Two novices, maybe thirteen or fourteen, wove through the crowd, trying not to spill their slushies on their robes. A fourth monk, potbellied and bleary-eyed, sat slumped beside a Buddha statue, dozing off as Instagram reels flashed across his phone. The monks felt incidental to the spectacle.

My brief visit to Wat Arun one evening was hardly representative of how Buddhism is practiced in Thailand—by locals or by tourists. Religion is deeply personal, and despite the temple's iconic status, many Buddhists I met during my travels expressed their faith in quieter, more individual ways: keeping a shrine at home, giving alms to monks, visiting temples on significant occasions, and striving to live with compassion, mindfulness, and moral integrity. The role of Wat Arun—and temples like it—reveals less about everyday religious practice and more about the evolving place of temples in Thai culture and the economy. They are tourist destinations, national symbols, and economic engines. Temples are the palaces of Thailand: its forts, cathedrals, and museums. Rising from the earth and reaching toward the sky, the golden spires of Thailand's most prominent temples are both earthly and celestial. While Buddhist temples across the region may rival them in wealth or scale, the density, grandeur, and architectural ambition of Thailand's temples set it apart within the Theravada world.

In 2024, Thailand welcomed 24 million visitors; more than 3 million of them visited Wat Pho, just across the Chao Phraya River from Wat Arun. This transformation inevitably affects the monks who live and work within these spaces—and their responses, ranging from complicity to resistance, are now playing out in newspaper headlines.

As I walked out of Wat Arun, I passed posters of monks with biographies printed beside their faces, like campaign ads. Their smiles were serene, their eyes digitally sharpened. In other images, they posed with prominent Thai business families. But it wasn't just celebrities who got to have their pictures on the temple walls. "Anyone who donates 1 million baht[$30,000] can ask for a space," said Suchada Phoisaat, an award-winning Thai journalist based in Bangkok. The images underscored the practical ties between monasteries and money. Wat Arun's endurance owed not only to public donations or entrance fees. Like many major Buddhist sites in Thailand, it survived on tax exemptions, corporate giving, and royal patronage. "Do what you want," said Phoisaat, describing the monks' attitude to the rampant commercialization of Buddhism. "But please donate. Temples suck money out of people."

Later that week, I stopped by a bookstore in Dusit, a trendy district in the heart of Bangkok. Piped jazz filled the room. A young man in high-waisted trousers, a crisp cotton shirt, and black loafers stood by a shelf lined with Russian short stories.

His name was Saharat Sukhamla, a twenty-four-year-old philosophy student who was still adjusting to life outside the monkhood. On hot days, he liked to retreat to this quiet bookshop where he knew the owners—and their numerous cats—by name. He'd browse the shelves, sip iced coffee, and talk about travel. London intrigued him. New York felt too far. He dreamed of taking his girlfriend to Bali. There was just one subject they tended to avoid: the reason he was no longer a monk.

Sukhamla had been adopted as a child by a farming family in northern Thailand. Because they couldn't afford to care for him, he was ordained at a monastery in Thonburi, on the banks of the Chao Phraya. Monastic life had been eye-opening, he told me. His abbot was kind, but others were not. Some monks bullied the novices, beat them, and, sexually abused them. When Sukhamla tried to speak up, no one listened. "People revere monks," he said, shaking his head. "But how can a country be healthy," he asked, "when even its most spiritual figures behave like this?"

On November 21, 2020, Sukhamla joined a pro-democracy protest in central Bangkok. Offered the chance to speak, the novice monk addressed the crowd on the importance of questioning authority. "When you enter a temple, you often hear monks preach," he began, his voice trembling with anxiety. He knew he was courting danger. There was no need to spell out that these sermons typically praised the monarchy—that much was understood. "But you never ask whether what they teach is truly correct. Why do we only speak of the king's virtues? Why don't we discuss the dangers of the king?"

For that speech, Sukhamla was arrested and charged under Section 112—Thailand's lèse-majesté law—which punishes criticism of the monarchy with up to fifteen years in prison.

Thailand was never colonized by a European power, never subjected to colonial extraction, nor forced to adopt Western racial or religious hierarchies. Unlike Sri Lanka and Myanmar, it avoided civil war and genocide. Yet, the Thai people have arguably never been fully free. They are legally bound to revere the monarchy, and their democratic system has been repeatedly interrupted by military coups—eighteen since 1932, when the country transitioned from absolute to constitutional monarchy. Over the decades, the military has steadily consolidated its power. In March 2019, Thailand held its first election in five years, but the military retained control. Retired General Prayut Chan-ocha appointed himself prime minister and rewrote the constitution to strengthen his hold on the state.

The pro-democracy protests that followed marked a pivotal moment. They began in high summer, led by students who gathered in Bangkok and other major cities. Their slogan, "Resign, Rewrite, Reform," represented their core demands: the resignation of the prime minister, pro-democracy amendments to the constitution, and greater accountability for the monarchy. Protesters accused King Maha Vajiralongkorn Bodindradebayavarangkun of using public funds to support a lavish lifestyle.

The king had ascended to the throne after the death of his father, King Bhumibol Adulyadej, and was a controversial figure. Where Bhumibol was revered for his gravity and dignity—widely seen as a Buddha-to-be—Vajiralongkorn was a polarizing figure, ridiculed in the Western press for his playboy reputation, penchant for crop tops, and for bestowing the rank of air chief marshal on his pet poodle, Fufu. Since taking the throne in 2019, he has tightened his grip on power by placing elite military units under his direct command and seizing personal control of the monarchy's vast financial empire.

By the summer of 2020, hundreds of thousands of protesters across the country were openly defying the monarchy. They compared the king to a giant monitor lizard, and parodied his sex life. When the royal motorcade passed through Bangkok one evening, students raised a three-fingered salute, a symbol of defiance popularized by *The Hunger Games*. One protest sign read: "No God, No King, Only Human." Thai authorities, having learned from earlier mass protests, deployed riot police who kicked and punched people, fired chemical-laced water cannons, and arrested dozens on draconian charges ranging from sedition to lèse-majesté. The monk Sukhamla was almost immediately sent to prison.

Thailand is defined by a sacred trinity: nation, religion, and the monarchy. The relationship between the three is close-knit—and insular. Rather than being integrated into society or accountable to ordinary people, the trinity operates in a closed loop, concerned primarily with its own preservation and advancement. At the very top sits the king, whose carefully cultivated image of benevolent temperance masks the reality: He is the most powerful person in Thailand, and he does not brook dissent. "When the current king ascended the throne, he imprisoned senior monks and stripped them of their robes," said Sulak Sivaraksa, a prominent social critic with whom I spent an afternoon in Bangkok. Now ninety-three, Sivaraksa has been charged or arrested for his remarks about the monarchy so often that he's lost count. "One monk even fled to Germany," he said. "Today in Thailand, no monk dares speak out against the monarch."

In 2018, two years before mass protests erupted, the king quietly assumed control over the Sangha Council—the governing body of Thai Buddhism. It was a strategic move. Monks in Thailand are not distant religious figures; they are woven into the rhythms of daily life. They collect alms at dawn, preach to temple crowds, and receive offerings of merit—donations made by laypeople to accumulate good karma. A single word from a respected monk can ripple through entire communities. By taking over the council, the king gained the power to appoint or dismiss its members at will—tightening his grip on one of the country's most trusted institutions. This gives him influence over more than 41,000 temples and 200,000 monks nationwide.

The hierarchy is evident in public rituals. In Myanmar, monks are seated above the military. In Thailand, it is the king, then the royal family—and only then the monks.

Unlike in Sri Lanka, Thai monks are barred from voting, running for office, or expressing political views. In return, they receive benefits: free education, healthcare, public transport, and tax exemptions. Temples, too, are not taxed, and donations are encouraged. The Vinaya—the monastic code—explicitly forbids monks from handling money or asking laypeople to manage it on their behalf. But in practice, this has created a vacuum of accountability. Corruption scandals within the clergy show that the rules are not strictly followed.

The entanglement of religion and power in Thailand has become increasingly difficult to ignore. In recent years, headlines have been dominated by stories of rogue monks caught snorting cocaine, driving luxury cars, and behaving more like playboys than ascetics. Some have faced far graver accusations, including the sexual assault of young novices. In 2016, police raided a temple where monks were breeding tigers for the illegal wildlife trade. They rescued 137 live tigers and discovered 40 dead cubs stuffed in a freezer. More recently, in May 2025, the seventy-year-old abbot of Wat Rai Khing—a temple actively promoted by the Tourism Authority of Thailand—was accused of embezzling more than $8 million in donations to fund an online gambling habit. When the money ran out, investigators said, the abbot began borrowing from senior monks, ultimately spending close to $15 million on gambling websites. "In Thailand," one report noted, "it can seem as though barely a week goes by without a monk being charged with drug possession, drunk driving, corruption—even rape and murder."

Such lurid scandals have consumed public attention, often eclipsing the slow-burning crisis in the country's far south. There, a decades-long separatist insurgency has targeted Buddhist monks in gruesome attacks—bombings, shootings, arson. At least twenty-three monks and novices have been killed, many while collecting alms at dawn; more than thirty have been injured. In April 2025, insurgents ambushed a truck transporting novices to a temple. A sixteen-year-old monk was shot dead. A fourteen-year-old was wounded.

The roots of this conflict go back to the early twentieth century, when Thailand annexed the independent Sultanate of Patani—a Malay Muslim kingdom—and imposed Thai culture, language, and Buddhism in its place. The modern insurgency began in the 1960s and seeks to liberate what fighters call *Patani Darussalam*, the Islamic Land of Patani. More than 7,700 people have been killed on both sides. Monks, as symbols of the Thai state, have become deliberate targets. The army now escorts them on their daily alms rounds, and many temple compounds double as military outposts.

The state's response has drawn widespread condemnation. One of the darkest chapters was the 2004 Tak Bai massacre, when soldiers rounded up Muslim protesters, bound their hands, and stacked them in trucks for transport to a military base two hours away. Seventy-eight people suffocated to death. Their families spent years campaigning for justice, but in October 2024 the twenty-year statute of limitations expired, closing the door on legal recourse.

And yet, even amid such brutality, the response from the monastic establishment has been muted. While the majority accept the state line, many others are silent. Only a handful have tried to use their moral authority to push for change. "The Sangha Council's response is minimal," said Budi Hernawan, an anthropologist who studies the conflict at Indonesia's Sekolah Tinggi Filsafat Driyarkara university. "A number of prominent monks in Bangkok are working with Buddhist and Muslim communities in the deep South," he told me. "They're collaborating with activists and academics. But the distance is too great—both the physical distance between Bangkok and Pattani, and the mental one."

That began to shift, slightly, during the protests of 2020. Among those who defied the monastic authorities was Phra Panya Seesun, a monk from Pattaya. "He took to the stage like a prophet," recalled Edoardo Siani, an anthropologist of Thai Buddhism. Reading from a smartphone, Phra Panya delivered a sutra with quiet intensity—a warning about kings and kingdoms that stray from the Dharma.

"At a time when kings are unprincipled (atham), state officials will become unprincipled. When state officials are unprincipled, brahmins and rich people will become unprincipled. When brahmins and rich men are unprincipled, the people in the city and the countryside will become unprincipled. That is how things work among humans. If those who govern behave immorally, the whole population will become immoral. If a king behaves immorally, the entire population will suffer." His words struck a nerve, and marked a rare willingness among monks to reclaim a moral voice in public life.

Those who do, however, pay a steep price. The young monk Sukhamla was sentenced to two years in prison and only released on bail after serving half his term. Under immense pressure from the police and senior monks, he eventually renounced the monkhood—a decision he found painful at the time, but one that ultimately proved liberating. "I was forced into the monkhood," he told me. "And that's true for many monks I know. But if you're forced into something, how can you truly care about it? In Thailand, we're seeing more and more poor, desperate monks—those who've been pushed into the clergy. What we really need are monks who *want* to be monks."

The Rebel Temples

A few days later, I took a taxi about fifty minutes outside Bangkok to visit what is perhaps the most controversial Buddhist temple in Thailand today, Wat Phra Dhammakaya. Sivaraksa, the activist, did not mince words when describing its leaders, calling them the worst example of the country's rule-breaking monks. "Their teachings go against the Buddha," he said sternly. "They tell followers that the more they give to the temple, the greater their reward will be."

In 2017, the Thai public watched in rapt attention as news channels broadcast a live raid on the temple, where the abbot, the famously charismatic Phra Dhammachayo, was charged with money laundering and receiving stolen property. Ignoring repeated police summonses and an arrest warrant, the abbot holed up inside the temple. It should perhaps come as no surprise that the disgraced monk had an ally in Ashin Wirathu, whose supporters rallied outside the Thai embassy in Yangon chanting, "May the teachings of the Buddha and Dhammakaya temple stay alive forever." In the overblown language that has come to define Wirathu's Ma Ba Tha movement, one of the protesting monks told the AFP, "If the monastery is destroyed, the Buddhist religion will disappear in Thailand."

When police attempted to enter the compound in the early morning hours of February 16, 2017, thousands of temple monks stood in the way. When they finally breached the complex, the abbot had vanished. Phoisaat, the journalist, who has deep friendships with several monks, told me that she'd heard that Phra Dhammachayo had fled to America, undergone plastic surgery, and was now living in Los Angeles. A bizarre rumor, I thought, not unlike the stories I was hearing about Wirathu—until I saw the temple complex.

The gigantic golden dome looked like something out of an Arthur C. Clarke novel. At the entrance, security men with walkie-talkies stood watch. After inspecting my credentials, one of them ushered me into a waiting room with a television screen. A film had just begun—its opening scenes tracing the origins of Dhammakaya. From the window, I watched monks in sunglasses gliding by in golf carts.

People I'd spoken to had described the Dhammakaya as a cult that preyed on the wealthy. Its followers were lured by the promise of learning an ancient form of meditation that would alleviate their stress. Once inside, they were encouraged to pour wealth into the temple. But here's why Dhammakaya raised eyebrows: The abbot claimed that donations didn't just buy merit for future lives—they bought wealth in this one. "The abbot said people who are born poor have 'stingy karma' from their past lives," a current follower told the British documentary show *Unreported World*. "If in this life you're tightfisted and not making donations, then in your next life you'll be even poorer."

"This may be Buddhism, but not as we know it," observed the documentary host, Marcel Theroux. "They say it's modern Buddhism for modern times. Their critics say they are a sinister, money-obsessed cult led by a rogue monk who thinks he's god."

The complex was a self-contained city spread across eight hundred acres, with immaculately kept roads, neat gardens, and gleaming high-rises. Donation boxes labeled *Path to Heaven* stood on every corner, each with a QR code for online payments. For those who preferred cash, there were ATMs. To be fair, the requests weren't entirely out of place for a Buddhist temple in Thailand. At Bangkok's majestic Wat Pho, which I'd visited not long before, donation boxes lined the walkways every few feet. The offerings read like a bazaar: bodhi leaves, candle molds, and lotus blossoms all priced at 20 baht (less than a dollar). For those seeking a more immersive experience, you could climb to the temple's summit or slip into a traditional Thai costume for 100 baht (about $3).

I was not permitted to speak with the few followers or monks present, nor was I allowed to inquire about the highly publicized raid and the subsequent disappearance of the chief monk. Once escorted into a conference room, I learned from one of several press officers—who flitted about me—that the meeting was being recorded for the temple's "archives." Before I could pose any questions, a press officer invited me to join him in a meditation session around the conference table. We sat there, breathing in and out, for several minutes. When I opened my eyes, everyone around the table was staring straight at me, their faces aglow with radiant smiles.

The Dhammakaya is one of several reformist movements that emerged in response to the needs of Thailand's growing middle class in the 1970s and '80s. For these educated and aspirational people, the old ways felt outdated. Thai society was transitioning from agriculture to industrialization, from tradition to modernity, and while the new middle class could still admire those who renounced the world, they didn't necessarily want to emulate them, observes the scholar Rachelle M. Scott. "The unabashed display of wealth by [the Dhammakaya Temple's] monastic leaders, who travel in luxury automobiles and wear imported Swiss robes, and its conspicuous honoring of generous donors with titles and special perks," resonated with this new middle class, Scott writes. They didn't see why they should judge monks for having the very things they wanted.

Later that week, I met with Phoisaat to get a better understanding of what I was seeing. I told her the challenges facing the Thai monkhood were completely different from anything I'd encountered in Sri Lanka or Myanmar. Thai monks seemed to be acting out, I said—seeking a release valve in the form of drugs, money, and sex. And with the Sangha's total submission to the monarchy, it seemed unlikely they'd push back against the forces reshaping Buddhism today. "Has it always been like this?" I asked.

Phoisaat shook her head grimly. "It was big-time different," she said.

When she was a child, Phoisaat's grandmother and mother had taught her that being a Buddhist meant praying, bowing to monks, and sharing food with them. Temple visits happened organically—when and if one could make the time—and donations were supposed to be within one's means. "Now Buddhism has gone big," she said. "There's competition to see who can donate more money. All this does is create envy and inequality. And it's made us all subordinate to the temple. And in line with how much they're giving, people also want more from the temple. We used to go to the local temple—small, very simple. Now people want their temples to be fancy, with air-conditioning, toilets, parking, seating."

Phoisaat suggested that the problem was twofold. First, there were the monks themselves—many of whom, she observed, had not joined the clergy for spiritual reasons but for earthly ones. This echoed what the former monk Sukhamla had told me: that some men became monks simply because their families couldn't afford to support them. What Phoisaat had witnessed was even more troubling. "Just this morning I saw a monk whose arms were covered with graphic tattoos," she said. Such markings, she noted, often identified former convicts. Her research indicated that this was becoming increasingly common. "The food is free, the room is free, and you have almost complete privacy," she explained. "It's a good life. Then there's the money from donations—no one questions how it's spent. You can do whatever you want with it." According to her, some monks enter the monastery with existing drug addictions.

After all that, Phoisaat said there was a temple we should see. It was across the river, on the far side of Bangkok, where the buildings were older, the crowds thinner, and the rituals less polished. A place, she said, that hadn't let go of everything.

The Santi Asoke was a Theravada sect like Dhammakaya, but it could not have been more different. The temple grounds felt like a jungle lair: lush, overgrown, with a waterfall cascading nearby and soft sand underfoot. The movement was founded by a dissident monk who believed Thai Buddhism had sold its soul. Phra Phothirak railed against the lavish temples, the monks who smoked and drank coffee, the merit-making schemes, and the craven deference to monarchy. His vision of Buddhism was austere and unsparing. One of his first rules was that potential donors had to visit his temple at least seven times before making a donation, to prove their dedication.

A former TV host, art tutor, and songwriter, Phothirak had a booming voice and a dry sense of humor. He didn't just criticize the establishment; he confronted it head-on, founding a political party and leading noisy anti-government protests. In the 2000s, he aligned with the People's Alliance for Democracy (PAD), known as the "Yellow Shirts," to bring down Prime Minister Thaksin Shinawatra. His followers often clashed with the police and military, but remained strictly nonviolent. To Santi Asoke, a protest was not just politics—it was a religious duty. "There is a misconception that the Buddha only said nice things that fell easily on the ears," Phothirak told *The Bangkok Post* in 1988. "Once, after one of his sermons, sixty monks died suddenly because of the hard-hitting teachings, sixty resigned, and the other sixty attained enlightenment. No one has died or resigned because of my teaching yet."

Mainstream monks denounced Phothirak as a heretic. In 1989, the Sangha Council disrobed him for "defying and distorting" their rules. He then took the name Samana Phothirak—*Samana* means "ascetic"—and in some quarters became more popular than ever. Today, Santi Asoke exists as an independent monastic community, which is not recognized by the state-approved Sangha. Its followers wear muted brown robes rather than the bright saffron ones favored by mainstream Thai monks. They eat only one meal a day, and sleep on simple mats. They grow or make and sell whatever they can.

As Phoisaat and I explored the grounds, we discovered the source of the waterfall: It gushed from the base of a circular wooden building seven stories tall. The water poured into a dark green pool surrounded by glistening rocks. Zebra doves flocked. An elderly monk in crumpled robes patted me gently on the shoulder. "It's not real," he said, laughing at my surprise. Introducing himself as Moon, he explained that the waterfall, the tree, and everything else had been built by monks with the help of members of the community. They raised the money through donations and the sale of handmade organic products like shampoo and toothpaste. "The majority of Thai society is consumerist," he told me as we walked. "But here at Santi Asoke, we reject consumerism. We reject capitalism. And we reject Buddhists who embrace such principles. We want people to detach themselves from the desire to make money and become wealthy. We want them to live simply and sustainably."

Moon told us he liked to sit by the waterfall, making himself available to anyone who wanted to talk. It was part of the group's ethos of constant engagement, he explained. I saw what he meant a little later, when we passed a cluster of elderly laypeople studying Buddhist texts under the watchful eye of a monk. Farther on, we came upon a lively exchange between another monk and a group of laypeople. The discussion came to an abrupt halt when they noticed Moon, and the group dissolved into sheepish laughter. "They were arguing about politics," he translated with a grin. "And that's okay," I said. "Thai people think the two shouldn't mix," he replied. "We disagree. We don't take sides, and we don't want power. But we are nobody's slaves." He looked over at the group, which had returned to its friendly argument. "We talk about politics all the time."

Where Santi Asoke confronts the establishment with ascetic rigor and political defiance, Dhammananda Bhikkhuni offers a quieter, more intimate challenge—no less radical in a country where the Buddhist clergy remains resolutely male. If Phothirak sought revolution through spectacle and renunciation, Dhammananda does so through presence: Simply by donning robes never meant for women, she has unsettled centuries of religious tradition. Now eighty-one, she is a revered figure among Thai women who see in her not just a monastic, but a pioneer.

When the rain let up one morning, I booked a Grab—Southeast Asia's answer to Uber—and, with Phoisaat, set out on the fifty-six-kilometer journey to a temple in Nakhon Pathom province, west of Bangkok.

On the way, Phoisaat and I continued our ongoing conversation about Thai Buddhism's uneasy present. In the wake of the scandals, she said, there was a growing crisis of faith—not just in monks or temples, but in the religion itself. Even the country's thriving amulet economy, once firmly rooted in Buddhist iconography and worth billions of baht annually, had shifted. People were now turning to what she called "strange creatures" to solve their problems. We passed one on the highway: a four-meter-tall demon with red eyes, golden fangs, and gargoyle ears. This was Kru Kai Kaew, a deity believed to bring wealth to his devotees. He had recently made headlines after reports surfaced of people buying kittens, puppies, and rabbits online to offer as sacrifices. Phoisaat looked visibly shaken. "This is not Buddhism," she said.

The road ended, for us, on the shoulder of a busy highway. A short distance from the traffic stood Songdhammakalyani Monastery. At its entrance was a statue of the Laughing Buddha. Though often mistaken for the Buddha himself, the figure depicts a tenth-century Chinese monk who wandered from town to town, dispensing gifts to children from a cloth bag. He is a symbol of generosity and abundance—an apt emblem for the monastery, which Dhammananda had built as a refuge.

In 2003, Dhammananda—then known as Chatsumarn Kabilsingh—became Thailand's first fully ordained female monk. She was in her fifties, married, and the mother of three sons when she realized that, despite being a Buddhist scholar, her contribution to the religion had remained abstract. She wanted to do more. So she asked her husband for a divorce. A 1928 edict by the Sangha Council had effectively barred the ordination of women by prohibiting male monks from performing the ceremony. So Kabilsingh traveled to Sri Lanka. When she returned to Thailand, newly ordained, she became a target of nationalist and patriarchal attacks. One journalist took to ambushing her in public with questions. But Dhammananda was hardly unprepared. Before taking robes, she had been a university professor, a Harvard speaker, and a television personality known for her feminist views. "They bombarded me with criticism," she said. "But I knew the Buddha would protect me."

Her composure likely owed something to her mother, a single parent who later became a monk herself. But because she had been ordained in Taiwan, under the Mahayana tradition, the act was dismissed by Thailand's Theravada orthodoxy. Becoming a nun in Thailand had never been a viable path. Nuns are denied the status of monks and often reduced to unpaid temple labor—cooking, cleaning, and serving tea, regardless of their knowledge of scripture. They are almost never the subject of headlines, unless by accident.

The monastery we now entered had been built on land Dhammananda's mother had purchased. Today it houses a modest temple, office quarters, and some residential buildings. Everything is funded by public donations—there is no royal patronage and no corporate sponsorship. Unlike many of the grander monasteries in the country, this one is quiet and unassuming, memorable mostly for the scent of blooming plumeria and the shade of heavily laden mango trees. A couple of dogs lazed in the heat; one clambered into a chair opposite me and stared.

A few moments later, Dhammananda Bhikkhuni joined us, assisted by a younger monk. She had a youthful face and an inquisitive expression. "For the past seven hundred years, when people speak of Buddhism, they speak only of men," she told me, speaking softly and deliberately. "Women are mentioned only in the context of making merit. But the greatest merit is ordination—and that's reserved for men. No one questions the imbalance, even though the Buddha ordained the first female monk. Why the fear?"

The word *question* caught my attention. It cut against everything the Thai Sangha expects from its monks. In Thailand, obedience is prized above inquiry. Dhammananda, it seemed, was suggesting the opposite—that obedience is precisely the problem. When I asked whether she believed Buddhism was patriarchal, she paused. "Hmm," she said. "It's true. I never thought of it, which is why I stopped to think. The Buddha was male, his immediate disciples were male. Yes, there were also enlightened female monks. In principle, Buddhism isn't patriarchal—but it supports patriarchy."

Sri Lanka remains the only Theravada country to officially ordain women as monks, though others—including India, Korea, and Taiwan—recognize bhikkhuni ordination. In Thailand, the Sangha Council has shown little interest in revisiting its position. "They don't want to share the cake," Dhammananda said. "They're very comfortable. They don't want women to have the same status—the titles, the money, the proximity to the monarchy." Songdhammakalyani seeks to redress that imbalance by giving bhikkhunis a place to live and practice. But progress is slow. "I don't want equal rights," she told me. "Equal rights are all about control. I know male monks who want to leave the order because there's so much control. But I don't even have the right to an identity card. And they don't call me Bhikkhuni. They call me 'Mrs. So-and-so.'"

The monastery's social impact is quietly radical, but largely ignored by a press preoccupied with the scandals and eccentricities of male monks. More than two decades after Dhammananda's ordination, there are still only around 270 bhikkhunis in Thailand. Ten of them live here. "It's hard to sustain the monastic lifestyle when there's just one or two of you in each place," she said. The problem now, she added, isn't only the Sangha—it's also the women. In Thailand, many consider ordination only after retirement, in sharp contrast to men, who often enter the Sangha as children. By the time the women are ready, she said, "they don't have strength to do anything much. We just got a new entrant. She has a PhD in Buddhist studies, but she's sixty-nine. She told me she can type fast. Let's see."

The reasons women arrive so late are rarely discussed. Dhammananda's path is inspirational, but also daunting. The idea of confronting the Sangha Council—an institution with deep ties to the monarchy—is hardly appealing. And in recent years, another force has pushed women toward the order: economics. Many single women in Thailand find themselves unable to save for retirement and are no longer welcome in their family homes, where they are viewed as burdens. For them, the monastery is not just a spiritual refuge—it is a last resort. But these are also the monks whose presence, some believe, has created tensions within the Sangha: women who enter the order not out of spiritual vocation, but material need.

For women, it seemed to me, the situation was untenable. Those who wanted to join the order faced enormous obstacles. Those who succeeded were unlikely to strengthen the bhikkhuni lineage in quite the way Dhammananda had envisioned.

After our conversation, Dhammananda's niece took us on a walk around the grounds. The dogs were sleeping. The mangoes were ripening, or falling. In a corner of the compound, a bhikkhuni was folding robes with great concentration, her gestures slow and deliberate. Elsewhere in the city, the golden dome of Dhammakaya gleamed like a spaceship. Beyond it, in the scruffier outskirts, the monks of Santi Asoke were tending their gardens. Three temples. Three visions. And in each, a kind of rebellion. Maybe this was the real revolt, I thought—the insistence on another way. Still here. Not yet extinct.

Epilogue

One morning in Mae Sot, I waited for a call. A group of dissident monks had recently slipped across the border from Myanmar and were concerned about being overheard. Could I find a private space? A quiet café that rented rooms was eventually agreed upon—though they insisted on vetting the location first. "Wait," they said. "Just wait."

I sat in the dining hall of my hotel, surrounded by Chinese tourists—young couples, families with toddlers tugging at their parents' bathrobes. The air was soup; the aroma was jasmine tea. My companion, the photographer Aung Naing Soe, guessed that the tourists were using Mae Sot as a base to slip across the water into Myawaddy, in Myanmar, where safe streets and open shops still existed, at least for visitors. An hour passed before my phone rang.

At the café, a staff member led me to a windowless room at the back. Inside, a monk in saffron robes was picking at a savory pancake with long, delicate fingers. A pair of glasses hung from a chain around his neck. His name was U Waryama. He had emerged from the jungle only weeks earlier, after months on the run from the junta. Beside him sat an older man in a striped shirt, his hair dyed brilliant black. He didn't offer his name but told me he was a member of the 1988 generation, a student revolutionary who had spent ten years in prison. "Hard torture," he said, emphasizing each word. He had arrived in Mae Sot two years earlier and never left. Then the door opened again, and a younger monk slipped in, masked and watchful. This was U Tun Kyi, once of Yangon, now of no fixed address.

By then, I had been traveling through India, Sri Lanka, and Thailand for more than a year. The question that had propelled my quest—why were Buddhist monks turning to violence?—had begun to yield answers. For the nationalist monks, Buddhist values were a disguise for ambition. Others were too timid to speak out, or believed their words held no weight. They let the harshest voices dominate, and acted as though the problem would go away on its own. Instead, it metastasized. But what I had started out believing was an aberration was, in fact, something older and more familiar: The collusion of faith and power. The weaponization of religion. Not a betrayal of history, but its echo.

I asked the men around the table if I was on the right track. Aung translated. The older monk nodded. "If you want to chop a log," he said in Burmese, "you need a crack. The log is the Sangha. The crack is the anti-Muslim attitude that senior monks have instilled in juniors. The axe is the military."

The 1988 revolutionary shook his head, recalling the propaganda that followed the Saffron Revolution. "So much hate speech," he said.

"Propaganda didn't begin with the military," U Waryama said gently. "It began with ordinary people. Even with monks. When we were enslaved, we should have hated the British. Instead, we told each other to hate the Indians. We said, 'Do we want to become slaves of the slaves?' We taught people to hate brown skin."

"Not you," the revolutionary said firmly.

"No, no, not me." U Waryama laughed. "I didn't learn those things, and I never taught them. But you understand what I mean? We are all responsible for the things done in our name—good, and also bad."

In Burma, the British imported Indian merchants, establishing a minority in a Buddhist-majority land. In Ceylon, they favored Tamil laborers over Sinhalese Buddhists, sowing resentments that outlasted colonial rule. In Thailand, the Malay-Muslim south was annexed and militarized. Borders once porous with trade and belief hardened into lines of suspicion. Minorities became scapegoats. Occupation bred resistance—but not always healing.

In Ceylon, Angarika Dharmapala recast the Buddha as a warrior. By the twenty-first century, his vision had calcified into Sinhalese Buddhist nationalism, embodied by groups like the Bodu Bala Sena. Far from being a uniquely Sri Lankan phenomenon, however, Bodu Bala Sena extended its reach through strategic alliances with other religious nationalist movements across Asia. It forged ties with the Hindu nationalist Rashtriya Swayamsevak Sangh in India, and with Myanmar's Ma Ba Tha organization. These movements, though arising from distinct national contexts, now form a loosely coordinated transnational alliance of religious extremists, each feeding off, inspiring, and goading the other. Through joint conferences and shared political language, they propagate nearly identical messages: that minorities are not simply different but dangerous; not merely citizens, but interlopers; not neighbors, but enemies. In each case, violence is justified as defense.

"What was the purpose of the genocide," said U Tun Kyi. "To show the country it needs a military. Rakhine was chosen only because it shares a border with Bangladesh."

U Waryama coughed. "We are all to blame," he said. "It's the ego that destroyed us. The ego of I, me. My religion. My family. My property."

The ego and power—its lure, its ability to corrupt. Monks who had once renounced the world now sought to control it. In Thailand, Phra Dhammachayo promised wealth to those who gave generously, turning merit into a commodity. In Sri Lanka, Galagoda Aththe Gnanasara incited violence to win political influence. In Myanmar, Ashin Wirathu's friendship with the military had saved his life—and cost many others.

The 1988 revolutionary took a sip of coffee. "In my day, the only safe place to talk politics was the monastery," he said. "Students and monks worked together. Now? Yes, some monks want power. They want more of everything."

"They don't really understand Buddhism," said U Waryama. "They preach of heaven and hell. They talk of Muslims. But who was the Buddha? What is Buddhist philosophy? People don't know. Even the monks are unclear."

I mentioned Abbot Zero. Their faces lit up. On this point, they agreed: Abbot Zero was one of the good ones. The conversation turned to resistance. The drone operators in Karen State were all women, the 1988 revolutionary said admiringly.

 Resistance groups were gaining territory, the younger monk reported. U Waryama told stories: of a DJ turned soldier who had lost an arm, a boxer who lost both legs, a painter who had learned to fire a gun with one hand, a poet who carried a rifle. There were others, too. In Thailand, Dhammananda Bhikkhuni took on the Sangha Council to follow her spiritual path. In Dharamshala, the nun Tenzin Kunsel exercised her right to resistance by educating other women.

And there were the monks sitting before me—the men without a monastery. Though they had been forced out of Myanmar, they carried the resistance within them. They had participated in protests in Myanmar, and in Thailand they were still protesting by speaking to me, even though it would likely cost them. The junta had long arms; it had a long memory.

Their choices reminded me of a Jataka tale I had read years ago. In it, the Bodhisattva is a monkey king who stretches his broken body across the River Ganges so that his subjects can escape an attack by a human king. "Do not fear," he tells them. "I will save your lives. Quick—step on my back and run along this vine to safety. Good luck to you all." One by one, the 80,000 monkeys bow to him, ask his pardon, and flee to safety. But the last monkey in the troop has long resented his leader. Now, seeing his chance, he climbs to a high branch and hurls himself down in a final act of vengeance—striking a blow that shatters the monkey king's heart. The traitor escapes, triumphant, leaving the Bodhisattva to die alone in pain. With his final breaths, the monkey king says: "A true leader cares for his subjects without end. Their happiness and safety is his only goal."

In the Jataka tale, the monkey king breaks his body so others might live. The monks I had met in the windowless room had made a similar choice, giving up safety and status for the sake of what they believed. The question, I realized, was no longer how religion becomes a weapon, but whether its original values can endure. As long as there are people who choose to speak, when silence would be safer, surely something of that spirit remains.

FURTHER READING

The Robe and the Sword grew out of many conversations, travels, and long hours with books that helped me understand how Buddhism, politics, and violence have become intertwined. For readers who want to go deeper, these are a few of the works that illuminated the path for me.

ON BUDDHISM AND ITS PHILOSOPHICAL ROOTS:

Buddha by Karen Armstrong—a clear account of the Buddha's life and teachings, grounding them in their original historical and cultural moment.

The End of Suffering: The Buddha in the World by Pankaj Mishra—a searching, personal reflection on how Buddhist ideas continue to speak to the anxieties of modern life.

ON COLONIALISM AND THE BUDDHIST ENCOUNTER WITH MODERNITY:

Theravada Buddhism and the British Encounter by Elizabeth J. Harris traces the complicated relationship between Buddhism, colonialism, and nationalism in Sri Lanka.

Alicia M. Turner's *Saving Buddhism: The Impermanence of Religion in Colonial Burma* shows how Buddhism was transformed.

Sana Aiyar's chapter "Revolutionaries, Maulvis, and Monks: Burma's Khilafat Moment" in the collection *Oceanic Islam Muslim Universalism and European Imperialism* reveals how religious and ethnic identities were reshaped under an empire.

ON THERAVADA BUDDHISM:

Theravāda Buddhism: A Social History from Ancient Benares to Modern Colombo by Richard Gombrich—a foundational study that shows how a tradition rooted in renunciation became woven into the fabric of kingdoms, nationalism, and everyday life.

ON MYANMAR AND RELIGIOUS VIOLENCE:

Myanmar's Enemy Within by Francis Wade—an urgent, deeply reported account of how Buddhist identity was mobilized into a weapon of violence.

Thant Myint-U's *The Hidden History of Burma* offers a layered portrait of a country caught between past traumas and present conflicts.

Matthew Walton's *Buddhism, Politics and Political Thought in Myanmar* provides essential insight into how Buddhism and power have shaped each other over centuries.

ON SRI LANKA:

Sri Lanka in the Modern Age by Nira Wickramasinghe is a masterful history of the island's colonial past and postcolonial struggles.

Buddhism Transformed by Richard Gombrich and Gananath Obeyesekere—a landmark ethnography tracing how contemporary Sri Lankan Buddhism adapted and hardened in response to social and political change.

ON BUDDHIST MILITANCY, NATIONALISM, AND RESISTANCE:

Michael Jerryson's *Buddhist Warfare* (edited volume) opened an essential conversation about violence carried out in the name of Buddhism.

Iselin Frydenlund's work on "war monks" and Buddhist nationalism in Sri Lanka helped me understand the political mobilization of religion.

Melyn McKay's fieldwork in Myanmar brought alive the human cost of religious violence, especially for women.

ON HUMAN RIGHTS AND DOCUMENTATION:

Amnesty International and the International Crisis Group—whose meticulous reports on religious violence in Myanmar remain indispensable.

The Law and Society Trust (Sri Lanka)—whose courageous local investigations have exposed abuses often overlooked by international media.

ACKNOWLEDGMENTS

I am deeply grateful to Pankaj Mishra, whose wisdom and kindness have guided me for many years.

My thanks to the team at Columbia Global Reports—especially Jimmy P. So, Jaime Leifer, and Nicholas Lemann—for their unwavering support and belief in this project. I'd also like to thank Sujay Kumar for the thorough fact-check.

I was able to focus fully on this book in part thanks to the support of the Royal Literary Fund. I remain especially indebted to Steve Cook.

Many people gave generously of their time and insight as I navigated the complex landscapes this book explores. I would like to thank Sana Aiyar, S. N. Ganeshan, V. V. Ganeshananthan, David Gellner, Simon Lewis, Timothy McLaughlin, Melyn McKay, Richa Nigam, Suchada Phoisaat, Janejira Sereeyotin, Tenzin Sangmo, Bhuchung D. Sonam, Salil Tripathi, and Alpa Shah.

My thanks to Vanessa Gezari for her exceptional instincts; to Ellyn Toscano, Fatima Bhutto, and Colombe Schneck for their generosity; and to Rahul Bhatia for his steadfast friendship.

I was fortunate to spend time at two remarkable residencies while writing this book: the Hawthornden Foundation's Casa Ecco on Lake Como and the Can Cab Literary Residency in Catalonia.

Finally, my deepest thanks to Ulrik McKnight and Indira Freya McKnight—my most beloved companions. I could not have wished for better fellow travelers, in books and in life.

NOTES

INTRODUCTION

20 **"sought change in the deepest reaches of their beings":** Karen Armstrong, *Buddha* (Weidenfeld & Nicolson, 2000), 11.

21 **"Because of eating so little":** *Majjhima Nikāya 36: Mahāsaccaka Sutta*, translated by Bhikkhu Ñāṇamoli and Bhikkhu Bodhi, https://suttacentral.net/mn36/en/bodhi?lang=en&reference=none&highlight=false.

22 **"The very format of the first sermon and its Four Noble Truths follows a medical model":** Richard Gombrich, *Theravada Buddhism: A Social History from Ancient Benaras to Modern Colombo* (Routledge & Kegan Paul Ltd, 1988), 59.

22 **"he even went to the field of battle itself and intervened personally and prevented war":** Walpola Rahula, *What the Buddha Taught* (Grove Press, 1974), 84.

23 **"as being for privileged white people":** bell hooks interviewed by Helen Tworkov, "Past Lives, Present Issues: bell hooks on Buddhism and Love," *Tricycle: The Buddhist Review*, Summer 2022, https://tricycle.org/magazine/bell-hooks-buddhism-love/.

CHAPTER ONE

33 **"aggressively Sinhala nationalist, family-centered, and authoritarian":** Alan Keenan, "Sri Lanka's Other COVID-19 Crisis: Is Parliamentary Democracy at Risk?" International Crisis Group, May 29, 2020.

CHAPTER TWO

43 **"We need war":** Mian Ridge, "Sri Lanka's Buddhist Monks Are Intent on War," *The Telegraph*, June 17, 2007.

44 **"but in fact also to Buddhism itself":** Iselin Frydenlund, "Particularist Goals Through Universalist Means: The Political Paradoxes of Buddhist Revivalism in Sri Lanka," *Buddhism and the Political Process* (Palgrave Macmillan, London, 2016).

CHAPTER THREE

47 **"such is his karma—to engage in violence and war":** Tessa Bartholomeusz, *In Defense of Dharma : Just War Ideology in Buddhist Sri Lanka* (Routledge Curzon, 2002), 47.

49 **"Sri Lanka is the Dharmadvipa":** Nira Wickramasinghe, *Sri Lanka in the Modern Age: A History of Contested Identities* (University of Hawaii Press), 93.

49 **"Sinhala-Buddhist entitlement complex":** Gehan Gunatilleke, "The Constitutional

Practice of Ethno-Religious Violence in Sri Lanka," https://www.academia.edu/37434371/The_Constitutional_Practice_of_Ethno_Religious_Violence_in_Sri_Lanka.

50 **an "infestation":** Betsy Klein and Kevin Liptak, "Trump Ramps Up Rhetoric: Dems Want 'Illegal Immigrants' to 'Infest Our Country,'" CNN, June 19, 2018.

50 **Modi likened Muslims to stray dogs:** Deepshikha Ghosh, "Narendra Modi's 'Puppy' Analogy Sparks Political Storm," July 13, 2013.

50 **"termites":** "Bangladeshi Migrants Are Like Termites: Amit Shah," *The Hindu*, September 22, 2018.

50 **"human animals":** "Israel: Starvation Used as Weapon of War in Gaza," Human Rights Watch, December 18, 2023.

50 **"When they're deemed nonhuman, discussion becomes offensive, an affront to civility":** Omar El Akkad, *One Day Everyone Will Always Have Been Against This* (Canongate Books, 2025), 55.

51 **"'Sadhu! Sadhu!'":** Henry Steel Olcott, *Old Diary Leaves*, Volume 2 (G. P. Putnam's Sons, 1895), 129.

52 **"Olcott was welcomed as a political and cultural ally":** Richard Gombrich and Gananath Obeyesekere, *Buddhism Transformed: Religious Change in Sri Lanka* (Princeton University Press, 1988), 204.

52 **"the beginning of Sinhala Buddhist nationalism":** *Buddhist Extremists and Muslim Minorities: Religious Conflict in Contemporary Sri Lanka* (Oxford University Press, 2016), 22.

53 **World Parliament of Religions in Chicago:** "At the 1893 World's Parliament of Religion," The Pluralism Project, Harvard University, 2020, https://hwpi.harvard.edu/files/pluralism/files/at_the_1893_worlds_parliament_of_religions_1.pdf or https://pluralism.org/at-the-1893-world%E2%80%99s-parliament-of-religions.

54 **was frequented by Sinhalese Buddhists from all walks of life:** *Buddhism Transformed*, 133.

55 **what happened to be the 2,500th anniversary of the Buddha's attainment of Nirvana:** "Sri Lanka's Fearful Symmetry," *New York Times*, May 29, 1985.

56 **"I did not want to learn":** V. V. Ganeshananthan, *Brotherless Night* (Random House 2023), 13.

CHAPTER FOUR

57 **highlighting his role in inciting deadly riots:** Hannah Beech, "The Face of Buddhist Terror," *TIME*, July 1, 2013.

58 **"The sword at home is no longer for cutting jackfruit—sharpen it and go":** "From Burning Houses to Burning Bodies," Amnesty International, 2021.

62 **"houses are offered":** Zachary Walko, "Interview with Dilanthe Withanage," *The Diplomat*, June 29, 2016.

CHAPTER FIVE

68 **scam centers, run by Chinese warlords:** Hannah Beech, "On a Lawless Tropical Border, the Global Scam Industry Thrives," *New York Times*, February 27, 2025.

70 **"The monks dread particularly the fate of Buddhism":** Alicia Turner, *Saving Buddhism: The Impermanence of Religion in Colonial Burma* (University of Hawaii Press, 2017), 23.

71 **occupation of Burma served as a rallying cry:** Alicia Turner, *Saving Buddhism*, 23.

71 **"The urban Burmese interacted with this wide variety of interpretations":** Alicia Turner, *Saving Buddhism*, 18.

72 **"Indians were far freer":** Mira Kamdar, *Motiba's Tattoos* (Plume, 2021), 77.

75 **these measures contributed to an exodus:** "Timeline: Myanmar's '8/8/88' Uprising," NPR, August 8, 2013; "Burma's Path to Genocide," United States Holocaust Memorial Museum, n.d., https://exhibitions.ushmm.org/burmas-path-to-genocide/timeline.

75 **"Britain's obsession with racial classification":** Francis Wade, "Fleas We Greatly Loathe," *London Review of Books* 40, no. 13 (July 5, 2018).

75 **often referred to as the "8888 Uprising":** "Timeline: Myanmar's '8/8/88' Uprising."

76 **"I could not as my father's daughter remain indifferent to all that was going on":** "Aung San Suu Kyi: Myanmar Democracy Icon Who Fell From Grace," BBC News, December 6, 2021.

76 **her address thrust her into the heart of Burmese politics:** "Timeline: Myanmar's '8/8/88' Uprising."

CHAPTER SIX

78 **They returned with split lips, bruised genitals:** "Myanmar: September–December 1996," Amnesty International, February 1997.

78 **villages relied on a single crackling radio in a tea shop:** "Interviews with Ashin Issariya," George W. Bush Presidential Center, January 8, 2010.

79 **"were a peaceful domain without worry":** *Le vénérable W.* (*The Venerable W.*), written and directed by Barbet Schroeder, 2017.

80 **"When I fell ill, I was alone":** *The Venerable W.*

80 **"The applause could reach the sky":** *The Venerable W.*

81 **"Kala-Kala-Yaik-Yaik":** Sam Dalrymple, *Shattered Lands* (HarperCollins UK, 2025), 51.

83 **"I will make sure the *kalars* have nothing to eat":** *The Venerable W.*

83 **mob swept through the town. In the ensuing violence:** "Muslim Minority Attacked in Myanmar," *Al Jazeera*, November 3, 2003.

83 **By then, many of the Muslims of Kyaukse had fled:** "U.S. Department of State Annual Report on International Religious Freedom for 2006—Burma," U.S. Department of State, September 15, 2006, https://www.refworld.org/reference/annualreport/usdos/2006/en/38286.

84 **incarcerated in notorious Obo prison in Mandalay:** Kate Hodal, "Buddhist Monk Uses Racism and Rumours to Spread Hatred in Burma," *The Guardian*, April 18, 2013.

CHAPTER SEVEN

86 **protesting a fivefold rise in fuel prices:** Channing Magee, Maddy Mcdonald, Solomon Li, and Martin Oh, "The Saffron Revolution," n.d., https://sway.cloud.microsoft/aweHoAJgioDjKbRx?ref=Link&loc=play.

88 **"May all those living things be blissful and happy":** "Paritta: Self Protection & Self Prosperity, Make It Yourself," Dhamma Talks, n.d., https://www.dhammatalks.net/Books/Paritta_Self_Protection.htm.

88 **tears in her eyes:** Seth Mydans, "Protests Grow in Myanmar Against Junta," *New York Times*, September 23, 2007.

88 **"the violence [of the military] should be the last spasm of a vicious regime in its death throes":** "The Saffron Revolution," *The Economist*, September 27, 2007.

88 **"an exceptionally serious step in a fervently religious society":** Thant Myint-U, *The Hidden History of Burma: Race, Capitalism, and the Crisis of Democracy in the 21st Century* (W. W. Norton, 2019), 74.

89 **Dozens, some say; a hundred, according to others:** David Steinberg, "Globalization, Dissent, and Orthodoxy: Burma/Myanmar and the Saffron Revolution," *Georgetown Journal of International Affairs* 9, no. 2 (Summer/Fall 2008), 51–58.

89 **"I fully support their call for freedom and democracy":** "His Holiness Supports Call for Democracy in Burma,"

Central Tibetan Administration, September 24, 2007.

89 **Wirathu was released in January 2012, as part of a general amnesty:** Sarah Kaplan, "The Serene-Looking Buddhist Monk Accused of Inciting Burma's Sectarian Violence," *Washington Post*, May 27, 2015.

91 **"I think our way ahead will be clearer":** "Remarks with Aung San Suu Kyi," U.S. Department of State, December 2, 2011.

92 **"reinforced nationalist narratives and fears of a global Islamist threat":** "Buddhism and State Power in Myanmar," International Crisis Group, September 5, 2017.

94 **"Oooh! Look how many of them. Kill them! Kill them!":** "Burma Riots: Video Shows Police Failing to Stop Attack."

94 **repeatedly strikes a child lying helpless:** "Burma Riots: Video Shows Police Failing to Stop Attack."

94 **demanding his camera's memory card:** Thomas Fuller, "Myanmar Troops Sent to City Torn by Sectarian Rioting," *New York Times*, March 22, 2013.

95 **"You should save anyone who is in trouble":** Htun Khaing, "The True Face of Buddhism," *Frontier Myanmar*, May 12, 2017.

95 **"Try to keep the government out of regulating the internet":** "Google Boss Eric Schmidt Urges Burma to Embrace Internet Freedom," *The Guardian*, March 22, 2013.

95 **what happened was deliberate:** Francis Wade, *Myanmar's Enemy Within* (Zed Books, 2017), 215.

95 **disconnect between upbeat Western narratives:** "Google Boss Eric Schmidt Urges Burma to Embrace Internet Freedom."

96 **"Rumors of a Muslim harming a Buddhist woman or a monk igniting mass anger and bloodshed":** Thant Myint-U, *The Hidden History of Burma: Race, Capitalism, and the Crisis of Democracy in the 21st Century* (W. W. Norton, 2019), 165.

96 **Buddhist mobs across the country had killed more than two hundred Muslims:** Thomas Fuller, "Extremism Rises Among Myanmar Buddhists," *New York Times*, June 20, 2013.

96 **"When you leave a seed from a tree to grow in the pagoda":** "What Is Behind Burma's Wave of Religious Violence?" BBC News, April 4, 2013.

CHAPTER EIGHT

97 **drafting a set of laws around race and religion:** "Burma:

Discriminatory Laws Could Stoke Communal Tensions," Human Rights Watch, August 23, 2015.

97 **"They want to take over Rakhine":** *The Venerable W.*

97 **"In our country, you're just a whore":** Sophie Pilgrim, "Buddhist Monk Calls UN Expert 'Whore' Over Muslim Support," *France 24*, January 21, 2015.

98 **that included newspapers, cable television programs:** Aman Ullah, "Ma Ba Tha: Who Hate the Rohingya," *Rohingya Post*, June 25, 2019.

98 **pamphlets portraying Muslims as perpetrators of global violence:** Simon Lewis, Zeba Siddiqui, Clare Baldwin, and Andrew R. C. Marshall, "Tip of the Spear."

99 **Ma Ba Tha members threatened opposition politicians:** Aman Ullah, "Ma Ba Tha: Who Hate the Rohingya."

99 **pressured police and judges to fall in line:** Matthew Pennington, "Firebrand Monks a Powerful Force in Myanmar Despite Setback," Associated Press, February 6, 2016.

99 **enjoying "unrivaled freedom" during the elections:** Matthew Pennington, "Firebrand Monks a Powerful Force in Myanmar Despite Setback."

100 **"Muslims have been targeted, but Buddhists have also been subjected to violence":** "Suu Kyi Blames Burma Violence on 'Climate of Fear,'" BBC News, October 24, 2013.

101 **"Are you going to eat Bengali meat?":** Simon Lewis, Zeba Siddiqui, Clare Baldwin, and Andrew R. C. Marshall, "Tip of the Spear," Reuters, June 26, 2018.

102 **International observers condemned the violence as ethnic cleansing:** "Burma's Path to Genocide."

102 **Amnesty International called it a "scorched earth" campaign:** Simon Lewis, Zeba Siddiqui, Clare Baldwin, and Andrew R. C. Marshall, "Tip of the Spear."

102 **became prey for sex traffickers:** Rebecca Ratcliffe, "Who Are the Rohingya and What Is Happening in Myanmar?" *The Guardian*, May 17, 2024.

102 **Throughout the genocide, Facebook played a pivotal role:** "Myanmar: The Social Atrocity: Meta and the Right to Remedy for the Rohingya," Amnesty International, September 29, 2022.

102 **"We openly declare that absolutely, our country has no Rohingya race":** "Myanmar: Facebook's Systems Promoted Violence Against Rohingya; Meta

Owes Reparations," Amnesty International, September 29, 2022.

103 **her office circulated posts:** Megan Specia and Paul Mozur, "A War of Words Puts Facebook at the Center of Myanmar's Rohingya Crisis," *New York Times*, October 27, 2017.

103 **"Myanmar would've been far better off if Facebook had never arrived":** Sarah Wynn-Williams, *Careless People: A Cautionary Tale of Power, Greed, and Lost Idealism* (Flatiron, 2025), 240.

105 **later known as Bloody Saturday:** "Myanmar Security Forces Kill Over 100 Protesters in 'Horrifying' Day of Bloodshed," Reuters, March 27, 2021.

105 **"They are killing us like birds, like chickens, even in our homes":** Emma Graham-Harrison, "More Than 100 Killed as Myanmar Junta Unleashes Worst Day of Terror," *The Guardian*, March 27, 2021.

105 **on charges of sedition against the government of Suu Kyi:** "Myanmar Fugitive Monk Wirathu Hands Himself In to Face Sedition Charges," Reuters, November 2, 2020.

105 **"outstanding work for the good of the Union of Myanmar":** "Myanmar's Military Honours Anti-Muslim Monk, Frees Prisoners," *Al Jazeera*, January 4, 2023.

CHAPTER NINE

120 **"He took to the stage like a prophet":** "Co-opting the stars: Divination and the politics of resistance in Buddhist Thailand," *Journal of Southeast Asian Studies* 54, no. 2 (2023), 200–219. doi:10.1017/S0022463423000280.

CHAPTER TEN

123 **"If the monastery is destroyed, the Buddhist religion will disappear in Thailand":** "Extremist Myanmar Monk Wirathu Backs Dhammakaya Temple," *The Nation* (Thailand), February 24, 2017, https://www.nationthailand.com/in-focus/30307197.

123 **"then in your next life you'll be even poorer":** "Nirvana for Sale," Unreported World, YouTube, uploaded August 31, 2020, https://youtu.be/MYm1EbNs4sU?si=m_7DUHr_j_XaVhiY.

124 **"They say it's modern Buddhism for modern times":** "Nirvana for Sale."

124 **Donation boxes labeled Path to Heaven stood on every corner, each with a QR code:** "Burmese Riot Police Attack Monks," BBC News, September 26, 2007.

125 **"conspicuous honoring of generous donors with titles**

and perks": Rachelle M. Scott, *Nirvana for Sale?: Buddhism, Wealth, and the Dhammakāya Temple in Contemporary Thailand* (State University of New York Press, 2009).

125 **having the very things they wanted:** Rachelle M. Scott, *Nirvana for Sale? Buddhism, Wealth, and the Dhammakaya Temple in Contemporary Thailand* (SUNY Press, 2009), 52.

127 **"No one has died or resigned because of my teaching yet":** Marja-Leena Heikkilä-Horn, *Insight into Santi Asoke* (Fah Aphai, 1991), https://www.asoke.info/bunniyom/insight-santi_mobi2.html.

127 **"defying and distorting" their rules:** Marja-Leena Heikkilä-Horn, *Buddhism with Open Eyes: Belief and Practice of Santi Asoke* (Fah Aphai, 1997), https://www.asoke.info/bunniyom/openeyes.marja_leena2.html.

Columbia Global Reports is a nonprofit publishing imprint from Columbia University that commissions authors to produce works of original thinking and on-site reporting from all over the world, on a wide range of topics. Our books are short—novella-length, and readable in a few hours—but ambitious. They offer new ways of looking at and understanding the major issues of our time. Most readers are curious and busy. Our books are for them.

If this book changed the way you look at the world, and if you would like to support our mission, consider making a gift to Columbia Global Reports to help us share new ideas and stories.

Visit globalreports.columbia.edu to support our upcoming books, subscribe to our newsletter, and learn more about Columbia Global Reports. Thank you for being part of our community of readers and supporters.

In Defense of Partisanship
Julian Zelizer

Losing Big: America's Reckless Bet on Sports Gambling
Jonathan D. Cohen

The Milk Tea Alliance: Inside Asia's Struggle Against Autocracy and Beijing
Jeffrey Wasserstrom

The Fall of Affirmative Action: Race, the Supreme Court, and the Future of Diversity in America
Justin Driver

Why Live: An Anatomy of Suicide Epidemics
Helen C. Epstein

The Web Beneath the Waves: The Fragile Cables That Connect Our World
Samanth Subramanian